KPI Analyzes in the Emerging Markets

-

Investing in Africa, Asia, Australia, Central and South America

Bernhard Walther, MBA

I0490705

December 2019

Imprint

Bernhard Walther, 2019

Cover Design/Illustration: Bernhard Walther

Lange Straße 28, 03238 Finsterwalde

bernhardwalther21@gmail.com

Print: Amazon Europe

All Rights reserved

ISBN: 9781652605959

Disclaimer

The information, data, data analyzes, statements and conclusions published in this book are not to be construed as investment advice or as a recommendation to buy or sell securities. The author has researched and processed the data carefully and in good conscience, but does not guarantee complete correctness and does not rule out errors. The author points out that he assumes no liability for incorrect, incomplete or incorrect information. The author also notes that investing in equities, stocks, ETFs and other securities involves risks that may result in the complete loss of the invested capital. The generated representations and collected data may be used with indication of the source.

Content

KPI ANALYZES IN THE EMERGING MARKETS

-

INVESTING IN AFRICA, ASIA, AUSTRALIA, CENTRAL AND SOUTH AMERICA

Growth opportunities in the Emerging Markets

Although the MSCI Emerging Markets Index has moved sideways over the past decade, while the MSCI World Index has gained more than 100%, some private investors swear on the "emerging markets". One can argue with the greater volatility the emerging market index has compared the industrialized-country weight index. On the other hand, there is potential for development in the emerging markets, which the industrialized countries have already left behind. Nevertheless, it does not say that emerging market companies will take advantage of this potential. The growth potential of the emerging markets is increasingly being used by companies in industrialized countries. For example, in some annual reports of German companies, there are currently strategic orientations aiming at spreading in the countries of the emerging markets. Now, if the industrialized and emerging economies themselves are pouring into these regions, who will ultimately benefit?

An investor can certainly sit back and relax if he invests in one industrial-weighted and in one emerging-market-weighted ETF. On the other hand, there may be several opportunities among the emerging market companies for finding interesting companies that have not reached high valuation levels yet. Some companies from the industrialized countries may not be powerful yield machines, but relatively safe investments. At the same time, fast-growing companies in industrialized countries have proud valuation levels. The market recognizes the growth potential and prices in these informations. With the growing prosperity of the emerging countries, their occupants will also increasingly invest their money in stocks. This population knows its own market, already because of the linguistic differences probably better than the industrialized country investor. A private investor who can find good companies in the emerging markets, may find them at lower valuation levels. This book tries to find potentially investable companies in the emerging markets with the help of key performance indicator distributions. These analyzes will show, which key performance indicator values can be set for searching stocks in the emerging markets. Because I have analyzed the key performance indicator distributions over several years, companies with key performance indicator values, which are consistently above the average values, could be filtered out. Ultimately, this book can be used as a working and reference book for stock searching and key performance indicator analysis in the emerging markets.

Since I prefer a simple approach, my "definition" of the emerging markets is very rough. For my definition I refer on the region selection of the Onvista stock finder. It divides the world into the regions of North America, Europe, Africa / Middle East, Central and South America, and Asia / Pacific. The last three regions are those, that I will explore in this book as regions of the emerging markets. I completely ignore the fact that a country like Japan is not an emerging country.

Chapter 1: Valuation level

In this first chapter, I examine the valuation level of the emerging markets. I start by examining the most frequently used KPI, the P/E, for its distribution in the emerging markets. Afterwards I will also determine the distribution of the P/CF.

Methodology

I used the Onvista stock finder to collect the data for the valuation KPIs. I defined classes and used the stock finder to find out, how many companies fall into these classes. This data can be reproduced in detail in the attachement. In WALTHER(2019), KPI distributions were determined in the same way. There is a possible distortion of the resulting distributions, because companies could possibly belong to two classes[1]. Fortunately, the number of these companies is extremely small. In WALTHER(2019) the three quartiles were determined für several KPIs, amongst other things for the P/E and the P/CF. The data determined in this book, can be used for comparison purposes. There, the distribution was determined for the years from 2013 to 2018, whereby a data kink between the two 3-year periods 2013-2015 and 2016-2018 was determined[2]. For better comparability, I limit myself here to the period 2016-2018.

The rounded arithmetic mean over each 3-year period was determined for each class. The histogram was then created with this. The cumulative relative

---

[1] Cf. WALTHER(2019), p.26
[2] Cf. WALTHER(2019), p.108, p.144

frequencies can be found in the "cum. part. " With this data the distribution function can then be displayed. The three quartiles of the respective KPI could then be determined graphically. The 25%, 50% and 75% lines are also drawn for the reader[3].

The table can be used to find out what percentage of the companies fall within a certain KPI value range. An example of this can be found in the first table listed in the attachement.

The distributions of the two KPIs were determined for each of the three regions Africa / Middle East, Central and South America, and Asia / Pacific.

Africa/Middle East

At first the distribution of the P/E for the region Africa/Middle East is shown as a histogram. There you can see how many companies fall into a certain P/E class. The distribution function can be viewed after that.

Because of the class width of 5 it is not possible to determine the lower quartile here. But the data can still be used. At least one can make the statement, that the lower quartile is below a P/E of 5. I will later list the three quartiles together with the other two regions.

It remains to be said, that Onvista provides only few countries for the Africa/Middle East region. The website does not show whether there are no

_____

[3] For example, if you find the intersection point of the 75% line with the distribution function, you can read a certain KPI value on the horizontal axis. This KPI value indicates that 75% of all companies in the region considered have a KPI value that is lower than this graphically determined value.

listed companies in the other countries in this region or whether Onvista simply has no data on other countries of this region.

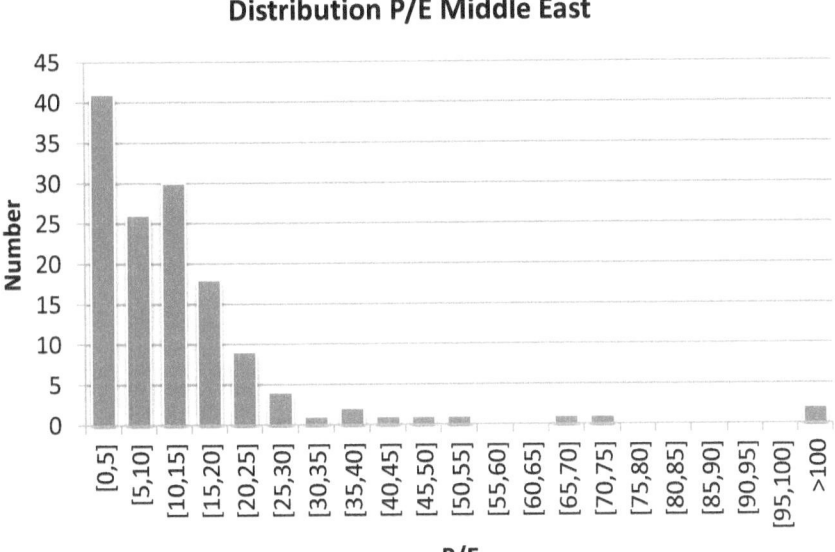

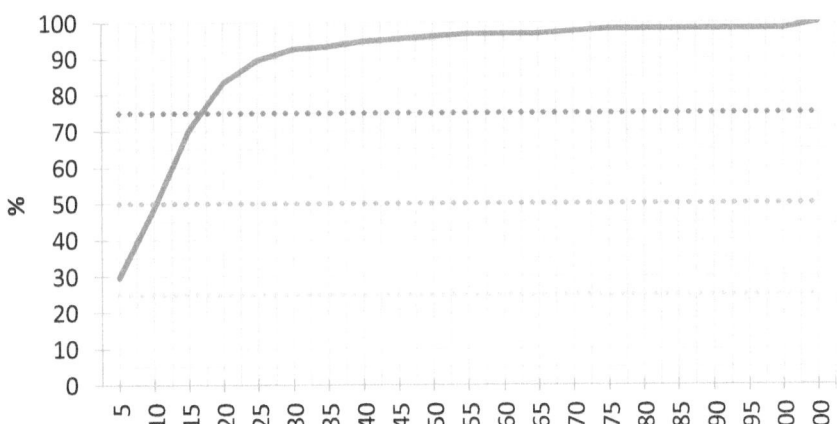

Countries for which Onvista can deliver data are Egypt, the United Arab Emirates, Uganda, South Africa, Saudi Arabia, Nigeria, Morocco, Lebanon, Israel, and Ghana.

Another valuation KPI should be consulted in order to better assess the valuation level. The P/B cannot be used due to insufficient data. The P/CF is therefore chosen.

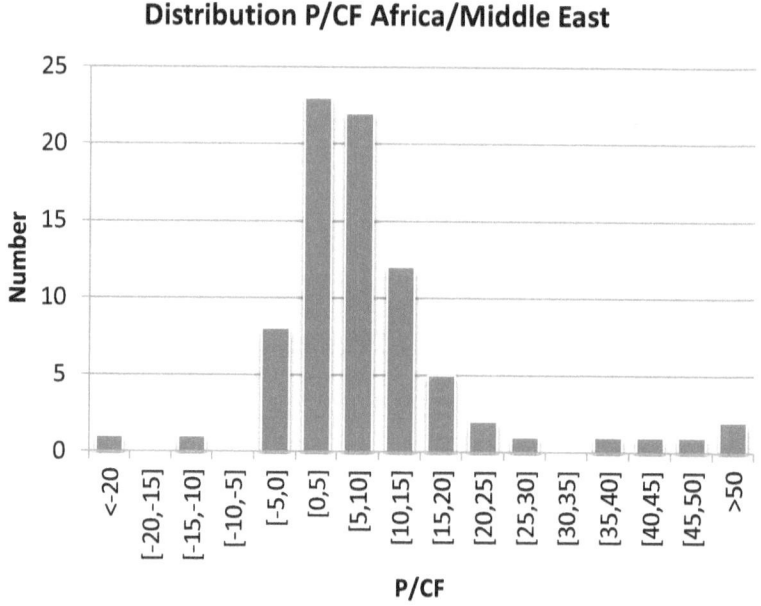

Distribution Function P/CF Africa/Middle East

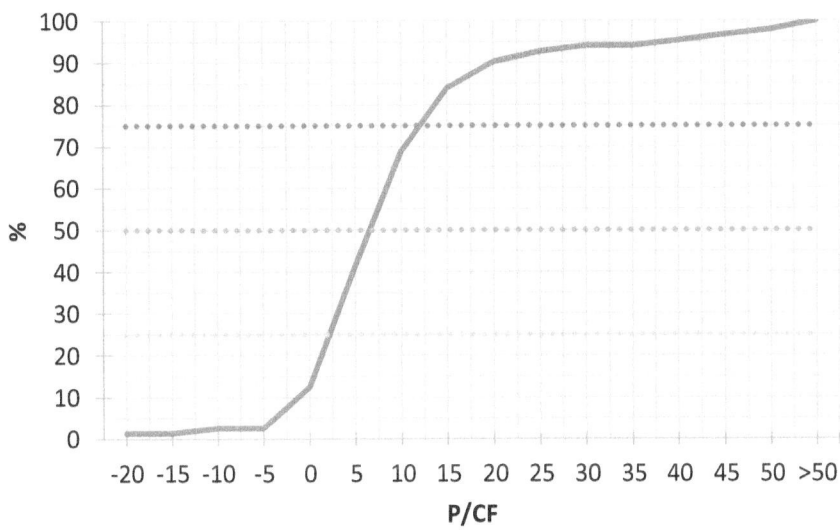

Compared to the industrialized countries for which the three quartiles of 10, 16 and 25 could be determined in WALTHER(2019)[4], the P/E for the region Africa/Middle East is in all three quartiles at least for the value 5 smaller. For the P/CF it could be shown, that the three quartiles of the P/CF for the industrialized countries (determined in WALTHER(2019) with 2.5 / 8.7 / 16.3[5]) are higher. It can be concluded from this that the valuation level for the region Africa/Middle East, at least in the range of the available data, is below the level of the industrialized countries. I have to point out that the reference data for the "industrialized countries" from WALTHER(2019) include the Asia-Pacific region.

---

[4] Cf. WALTHER(2019), p.111
[5] Cf. WALTHER(2019), p.147

Central and South America

An analogous investigation follows for the region of Central and South America.

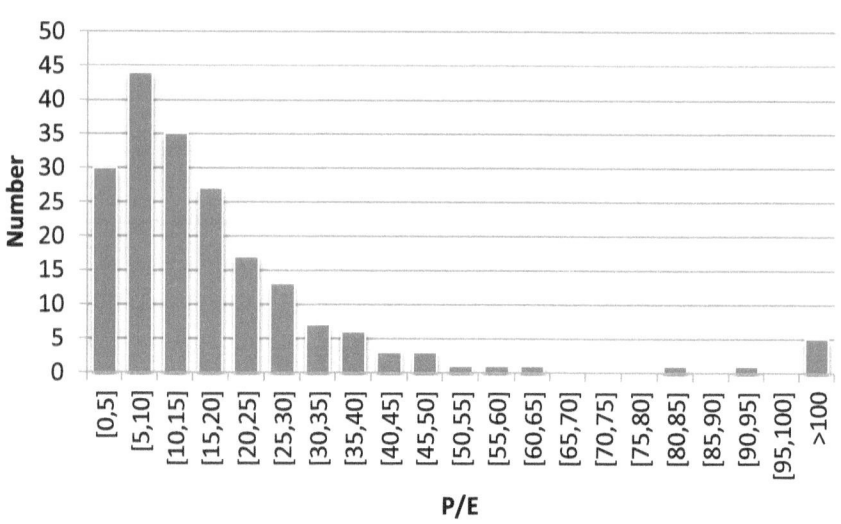

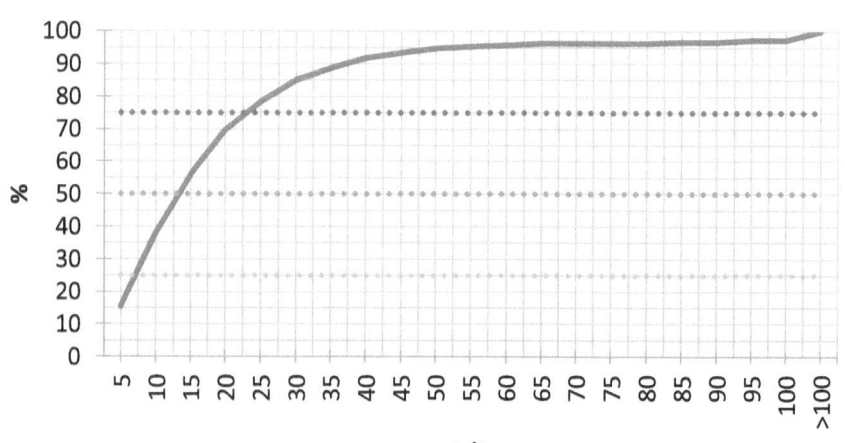

The P/E quartiles for Central and South America for the period 2016-2018 are at least 2 below the P/E quartiles of the industrialized countries. It is also striking that the P/E quartiles of Central and South America are at least 2 above the values of the Africa/Middle East region.

The distribution of the P/CF follows for better comparability of the valuation level.

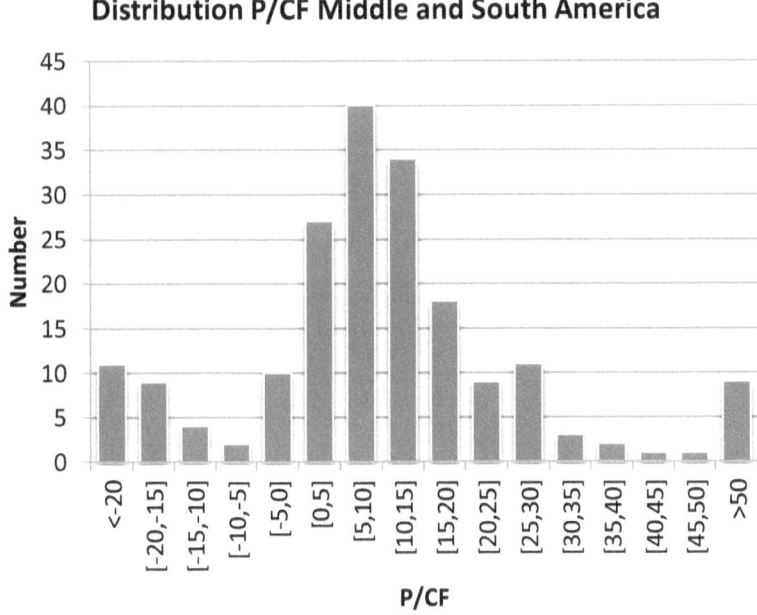

Distribution P/CF Middle and South America

Distribution Function P/CF Middle and South America

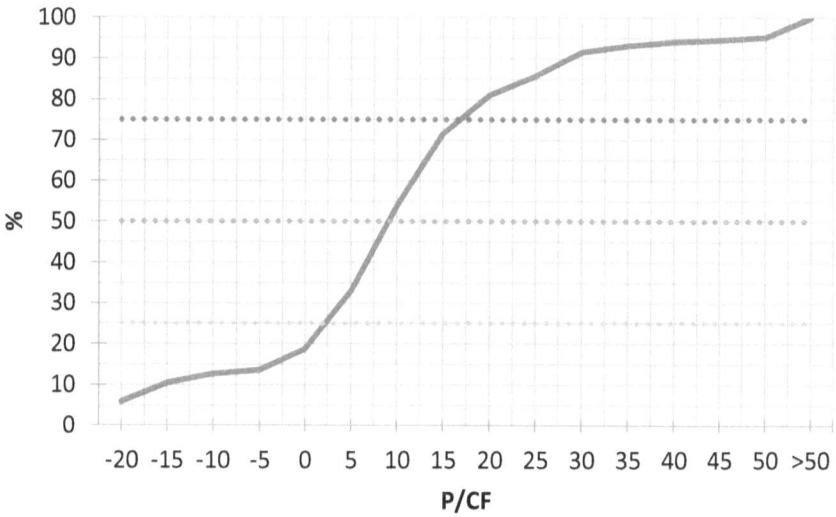

The insufficient data situation in 2016 was problematic when determining the P/CF. Therefore the diagrams were created based on averaging the data over the years 2017 and 2018. When comparing the quantiles with the Africa/Middle East region and in comparision with the industrialized countries, only slight differences can be identified.

Asia/Pacific

Finally, I show the distributions of the P/E and the P/CF for the region Asia/Pacific. The first thing that emerges from the analysis is that the number of companies, for which data can be found, is much higher than in the other two regions. As a result, the quartiles can be found close to the values for the "industrialized countries" from WALTHER(2019), because the Asia/Pacific region was included in the distribution analyzes there.

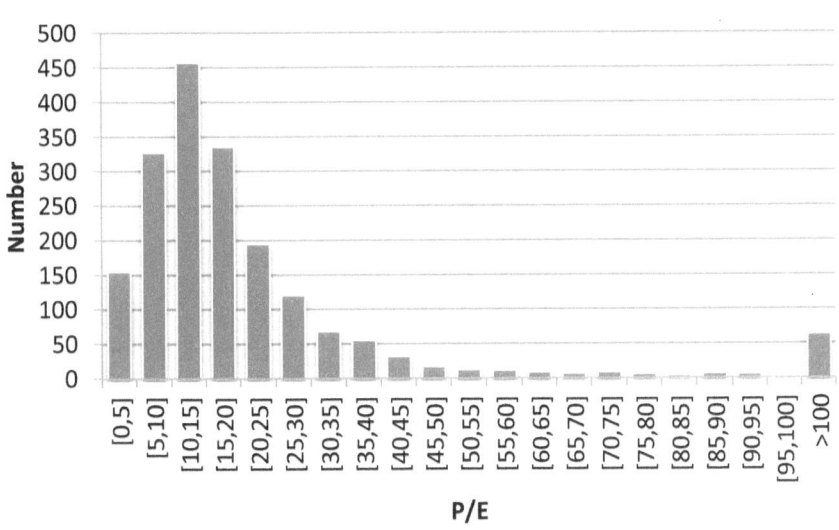

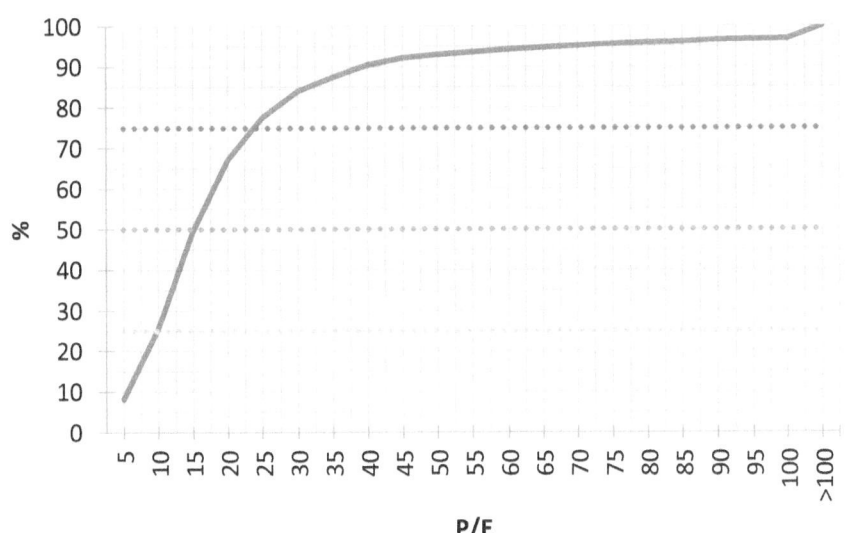

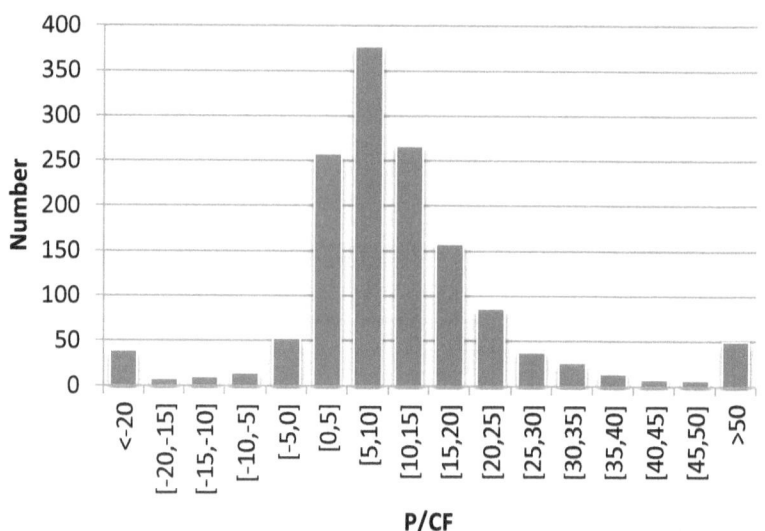

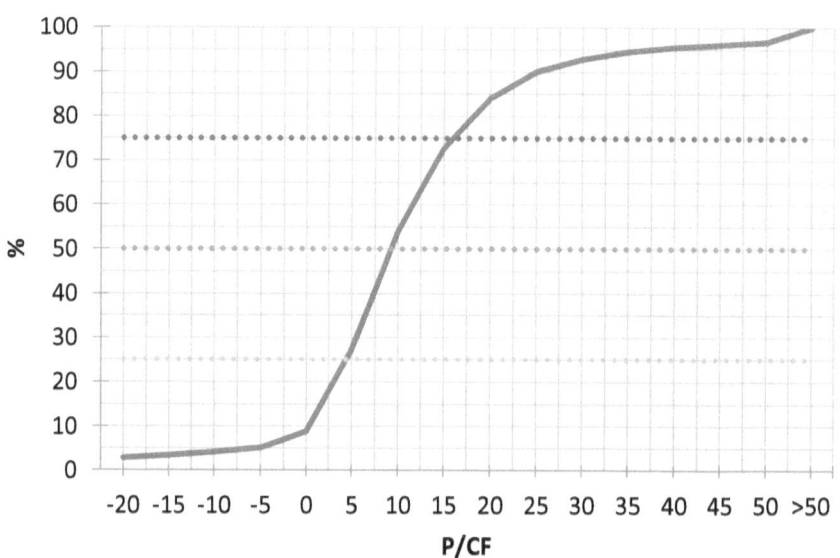

The quartiles are shown in a table below so that the comparisons already described can be clearly understood.

Comparision P/E quartiles				
quantile	Africa/Middle East	Mid./South America	Asia/Pacific	Industrialized Countries[6]
lower quantile	<5	7	10	10
median	10,5	13	15	16
upper quartile	17	23	23,5	25

Comparision P/CF quartiles				
quantile	Africa/Middle East	Mid./South America	Asia/Pacific	Industrialized Countries[7]
lower quantile	2	2	4,5	2,5
median	6,5	9	9	8,7
upper quartile	12	17	16,5	16,3

It is clearly regognizable that the region Africa/Middle East has the lowest valuation level. In contrast, there are relatively similar quartile values for the other three regions listed.

The inclusion of the P/CF as an additional KPI creates greater certainty in the statements. Because this certainty is now given to a certain extent, I will limit to the P/E in the next section.

---

[6] Cf. WALTHER(2019), p.111
[7] Cf. WALTHER(2019), p.147

P/E and Market Capitalization

To what extent the P/E or the valuation level is related to the market capitalization or the size of the company, I will show below. The underlying data can be found in the attachement. The investigations were carried out for 2018. The 2.5-lines are shown for the regions Africa/Middle East and Central and South America, and the 10-lines for the Asia / Pacific region.

For the region Africa/Middle East it is clear, that most companies can be found below a MCap of 4 billion € and below a P/E of 30. The P/E median for the lowest MCap class tends to be shifted downwards.

Distribution P/E-MCap Africa/Middle East

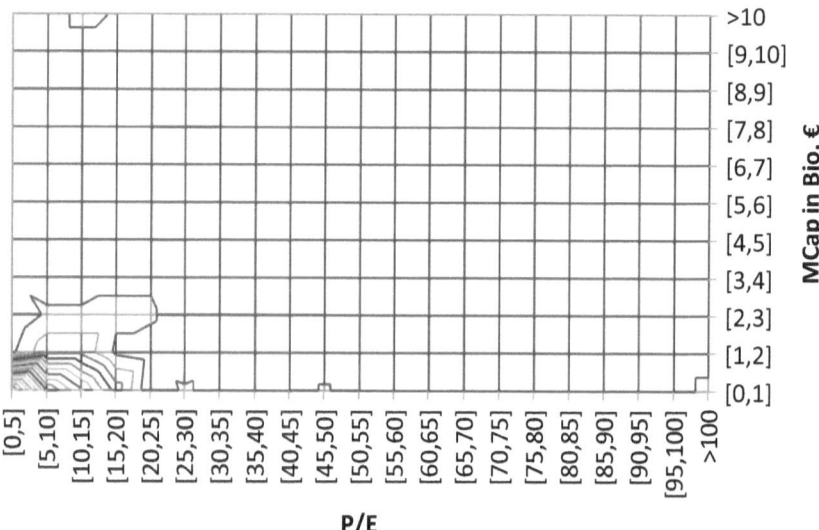

Distribution P/E-MCap Middle and South America

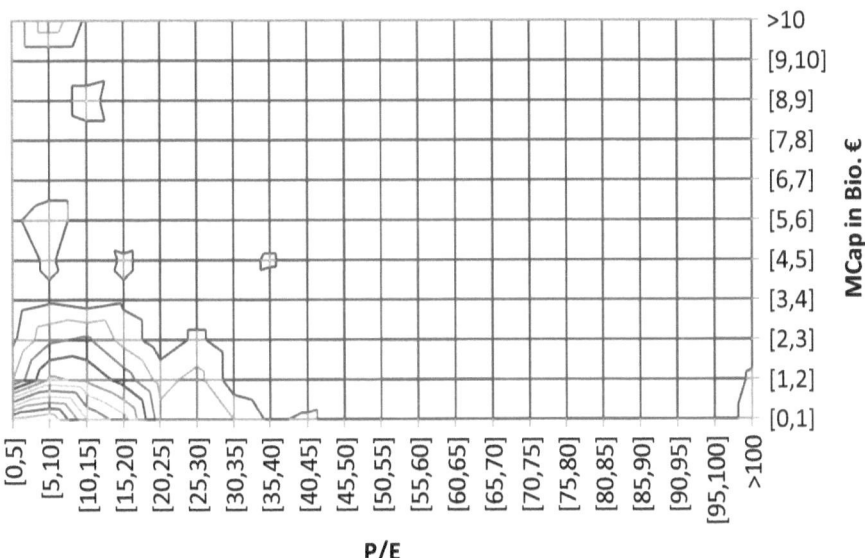

In the region Central and South America, the distribution of the P/E appears to be largely independent of market capitalization. Most companies can be found below a MCap of 4 billion € and below a P/E ratio of 40. The distribution of the P/E of the region Asia/Pacific has shifted a little further to the right compared to the distribution of Central and South America, just like the P/E median determined at the beginning.

Distribution P/E-MCap Asia/Pacific

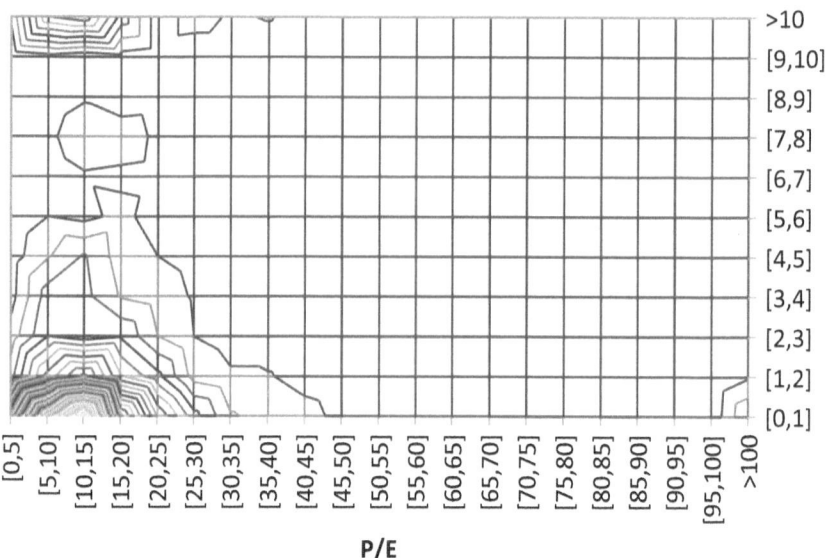

MCap in Bio. €

>10
[9,10]
[8,9]
[7,8]
[6,7]
[5,6]
[4,5]
[3,4]
[2,3]
[1,2]
[0,1]

[0,5]
[5,10]
[10,15]
[15,20]
[20,25]
[25,30]
[30,35]
[35,40]
[40,45]
[45,50]
[50,55]
[55,60]
[60,65]
[65,70]
[70,75]
[75,80]
[80,85]
[85,90]
[90,95]
[95,100]
>100

P/E

Chapter 2: Profit Growth

In WALTHER(2019) it was shown, that quantitative strategies based on growing revenues and profits can achieve good results[8]. A company will only be able to grow in the long term with growing revenues and profits. I will analyze below, how the revenue and profit growth of the emerging markets differs from the industrialized countries.

In WALTHER (2019), the three quartiles for revenue growth and for profit growth were determined as a mean over the years 2013 to 2018. I will list these later for comparison purposes. If you look at the data tables used there[9], the PG and RG values vary only slightly over the entire period. Therefore, and because the previous chapter also worked with the restriction to the period 2016 to 2018, I will limit myself to this period. A minimum market capitalization of 1 billion € was also chosen in WALTHER (2019). This should be taken into account in the following analyzes.

This chapter will be about profit growth. The following chapter then deals with revenue growth because a different data collection methodology had to be chosen.

---

[8] Cf. WALTHER(2019), p.26 ff.
[9] see WALTHER(2019), p.29 und p.32

Profit Growth Distributions

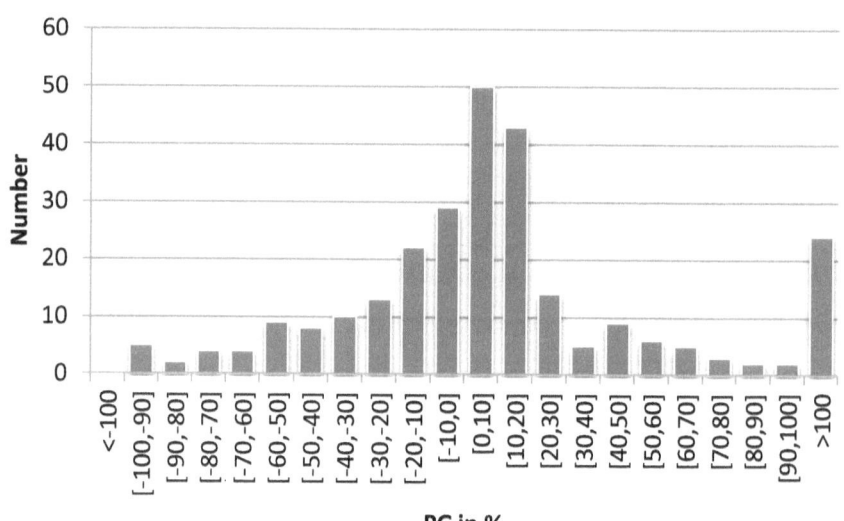

Distribution PG Africa/Middle East

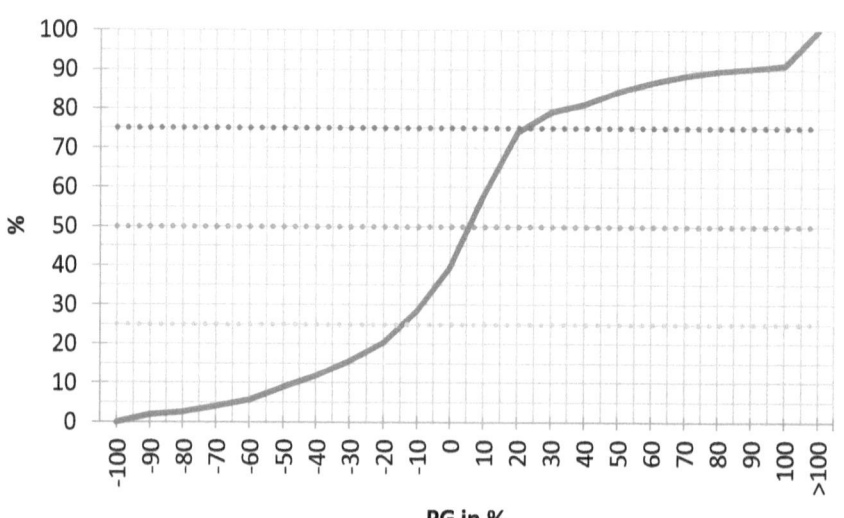

Distribution Function PG Africa/Middle East

Distribution PG Middle and South America

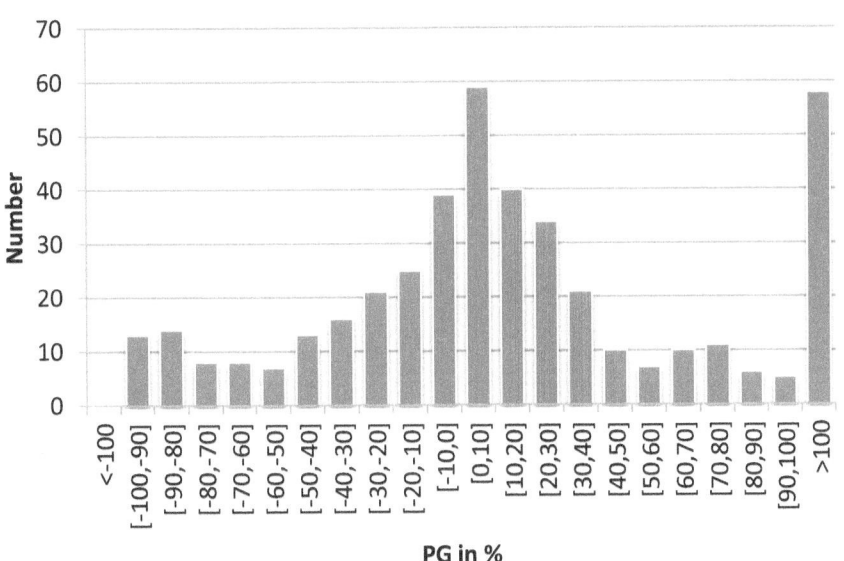

Distribution Function PG Middle and South America

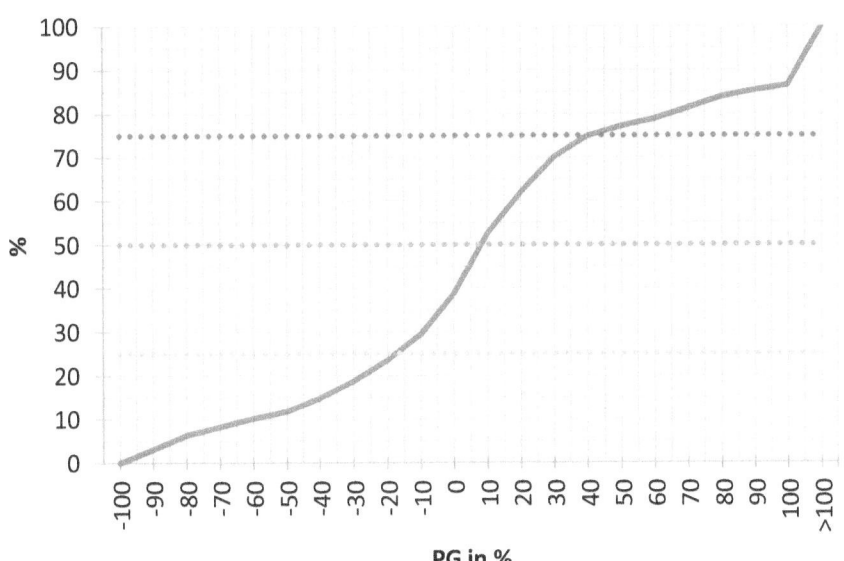

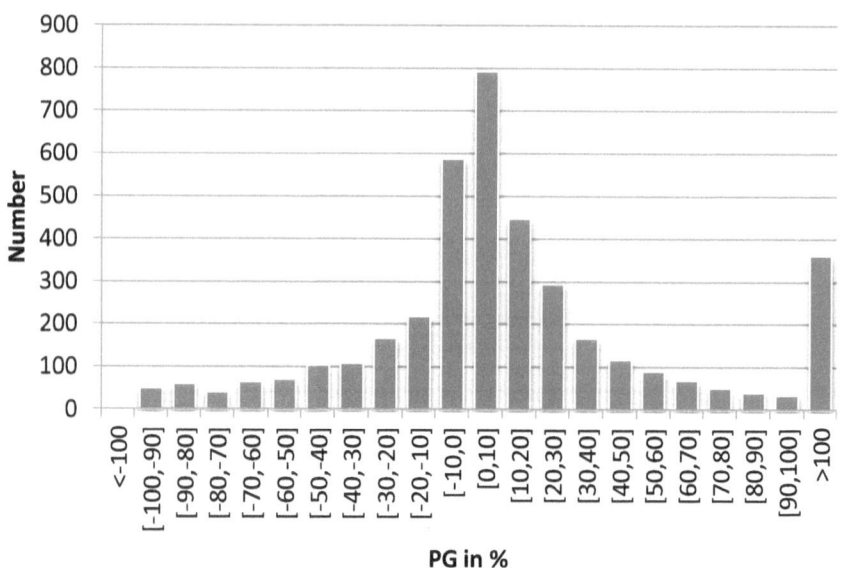

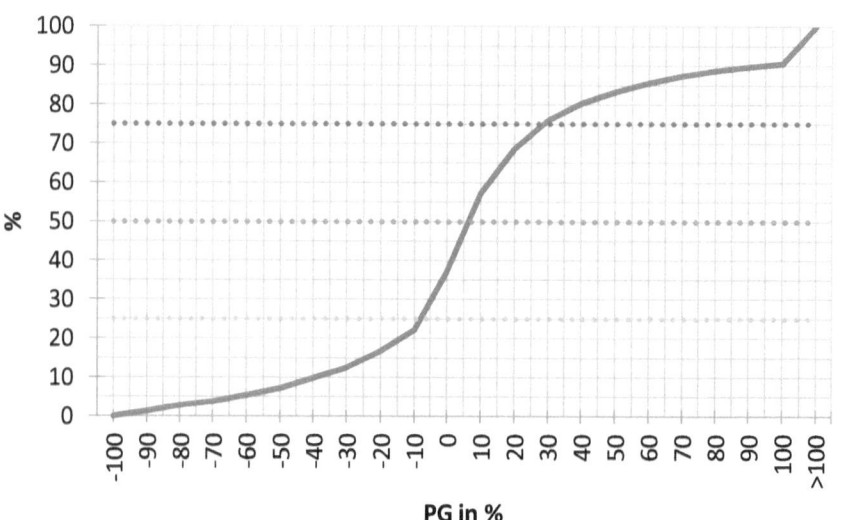

Comparision PG-quantiles (in %)				
quantile	Africa/Middle East	Mid./South America	Asia/Pacific	Industrialized Countries[10]
lower quartile	-15	-18	-8	-5,7
median	6	7,5	7	7,5
upper quartile	22,5	40	28	26

The PG quartiles for the region Africa/Middle East are each below the PG quartiles of the industrialized countries. However, the median of the two regions is not that far apart.

Overall, it is striking that the median has roughly the same value across all regions. The lower quartiles of the regions Africa/Middle East and Central and South America are significantly below the lower quartiles of the other regions. The upper quartile of the region Central and South America is higher than the upper quartiles of the other regions.

Unfortunately, the analysis of the distribution of revenue growth cannot be done in the same way. Onvista's stock finder finds very few companies for which a revenue growth is indicated for the emerging markets. First of all, I therefore investigate whether or to what extent there is a correlation between profit growth and market capitalization.

---

[10] Cf. WALTHER(2019), p.33

Profit Growth and Market Capitalization

Quartiles were found in each case. However, these may depend on the size of the company. I therefore look, to what extent there is a correlation between profit growth and market capitalization.

If you look at the tables of the PG distributions in the attachment, 2018 shows only slight deviations compared the two previous years. Therefore, I only investigate the relation between profit growth and market capitalization for the year 2018.

The bivariate distribution of PG and MCap in 2018 is shown below. For the region Africa/Middle East the 2.5-lines are shown. The more lines encircle an area, the more companies are within an area of this diagram. The underlying data can be found in the attachment.

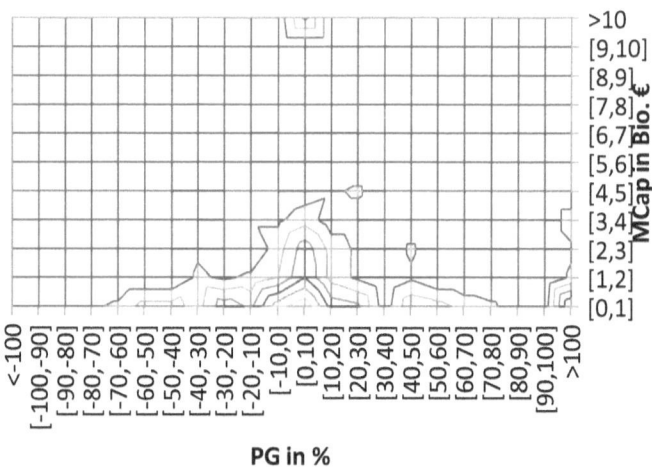

Diatribution PG-MCap Africa/Middle East

For the region Africa/Middle East, it is clear that the median is consistently within the PG interval [0|10]. The PG distribution narrows as market capitalization increases, but remains relatively symmetrical, with a tendency towards positive profit growth. As a result, both high and low PG values can be found in smaller companies in terms of market capitalization.

Distribution PG-MCap Middle and South America

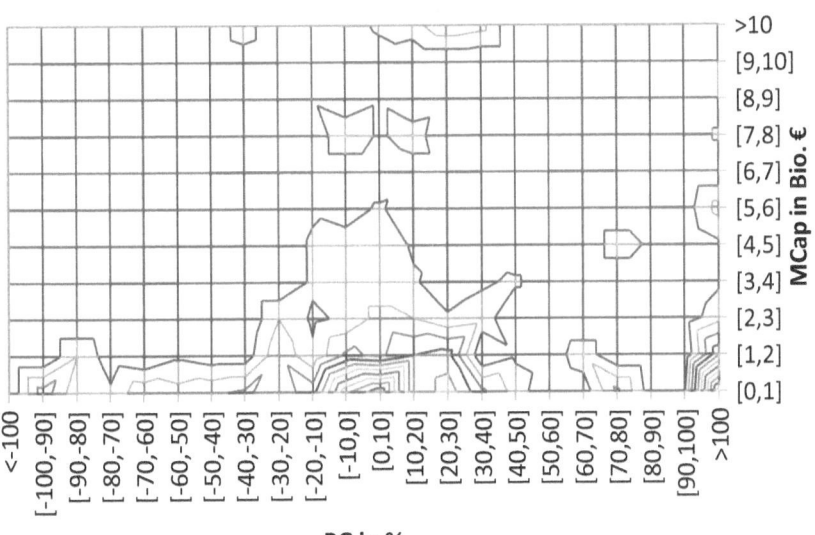

PG in %

The bivariate distribution for the region Central and South America is somewhat similar to the distribution of the region Africa/Middle East. There also is a median that moves within the PG interval [0|10], but here it is spread a little wider with a higher MCap. Due to the higher number of companies, the PG distribution appears broader, but also narrows with increasing MCap. The trend towards positive profit growth can also be seen here.

For the region Asia/Pacific, due to the high number of companies, 10-lines were used instead of the 2.5-lines.

Distribution PG-MCap Asia/Pacific

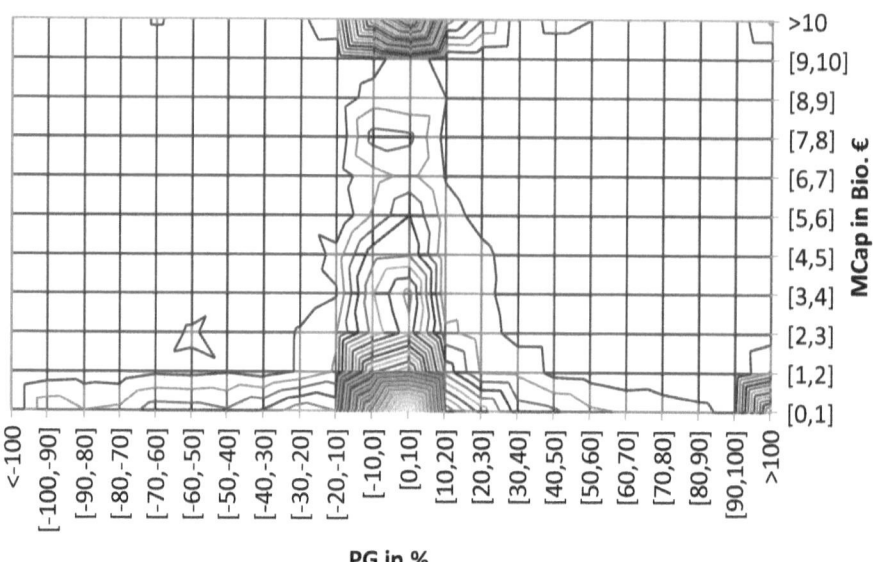

The PG median, apparently independent of the MCap, also seems to exist here. Likewise, a more symmetrical PG distribution, which becomes narrower with increasing market capitalization, can be determined.

Anyone looking for high profit growth of over 20 % will find it in the emerging markets. You do not necessarily have to search at the small caps. Mid-caps and large-caps with high profit growth are not uncommon here.

Profit Growth Continuity

But what about continuity in profit growth? As in WALTHER(2019), survival time analyzes could make useful statements about the continuity of a KPI value. I do not want to carry out such detailed analyzes as there. Instead, I am investigating, which companies showed above-average profit growth in the period from 2012 to 2018.

The companies listed are those that have achieved above-average profit growth in each year of this period. Therefore, it was checked, which companies met the PG median every year.

Africa/Middle East: PG-Median from 2012 to 2018 fulfilled			
WKN[11]	Company	Business Sector	Ctr.[12]
784554	AVI	Consumer goods	ZAF[13]
779555	Capitec Bank Holdings	Financial Service	ZAF
A0RPRJ	Clicks Group	Drug Store/ Cosmetics	ZAF
A0EACV	Firstrand	Financial Service	ZAF
907557	RMB Holdings	Financial Service	ZAF

Mittel- und Südamerika: PG-Median from 2012 to 2018 fulfilled			
WKN	Company	Business Sector	Land
940699	Grupo Financiero Galicia	Financial Service	ARG[14]
A2JKE5	Banregio Grupo Financiero	Financial Service	MEX[15]

---

[11] WKN – **W**ertpapierkenn**n**ummer – A number used in Germany for identifying listed companies.
[12] Ctr. - Country
[13] ZAF – South Africa
[14] ARG - Argentina
[15] MEX - Mexico

Asien/Pazifik: PG-Median from 2012 to 2018 fulfilled			
WKN	Unternehmen	Branche	Land
888201	Ayala Land	Real Estate	PHL[16]
A0Q10L	Beijing Enterprises	Services	HKG[17]
A2N0QN	Charter Hall Education Trust	Real Estate	AUS[18]
A0M4QS	China Shipbuilding Industry Corp	Ship building / armaments ind.	CHN[19]
A0M3VR	Tonghua Dongbao Pharmaceuticals	Pharma	CHN
A0B9CF	Tosei Corp.	Real Estate	JPN[20]

---

[16] PHL - Philippines
[17] HKG – Hong Kong
[18] AUS - Australia
[19] CHN - China
[20] JPN - Japan

Chapter 3: Revenue Growth

The data collection for revenue growth turned out to be much more complex. Onvista was only able to show revenue growth for few companies in the three regions.

For this reason, a list of companies with a minimum market capitalization related to 2018 was searched for each region on Onvista. The companies were then examined one after another on finanzen.net for their revenue growth. For few companies no data could be displayed on finanzen.net.

In the attachment the reader can find the list of companies, which provided the basis for the following investigations. The companies are sorted there according to their market capitalization in 2018.

Africa/Middle East

As the minimum market capitalization in 2018, I chose 1 billion € for the region Africa/Middle East. The distribution, distribution function, and quartiles for three years are shown below. Because the data from finanzen.net could be determined without great effort for all companies on the list back till the year 2012, the development of the distribution can be shown. I therefore show the distribution, the distribution function, and the quartiles for the years 2012, 2015 and 2018.

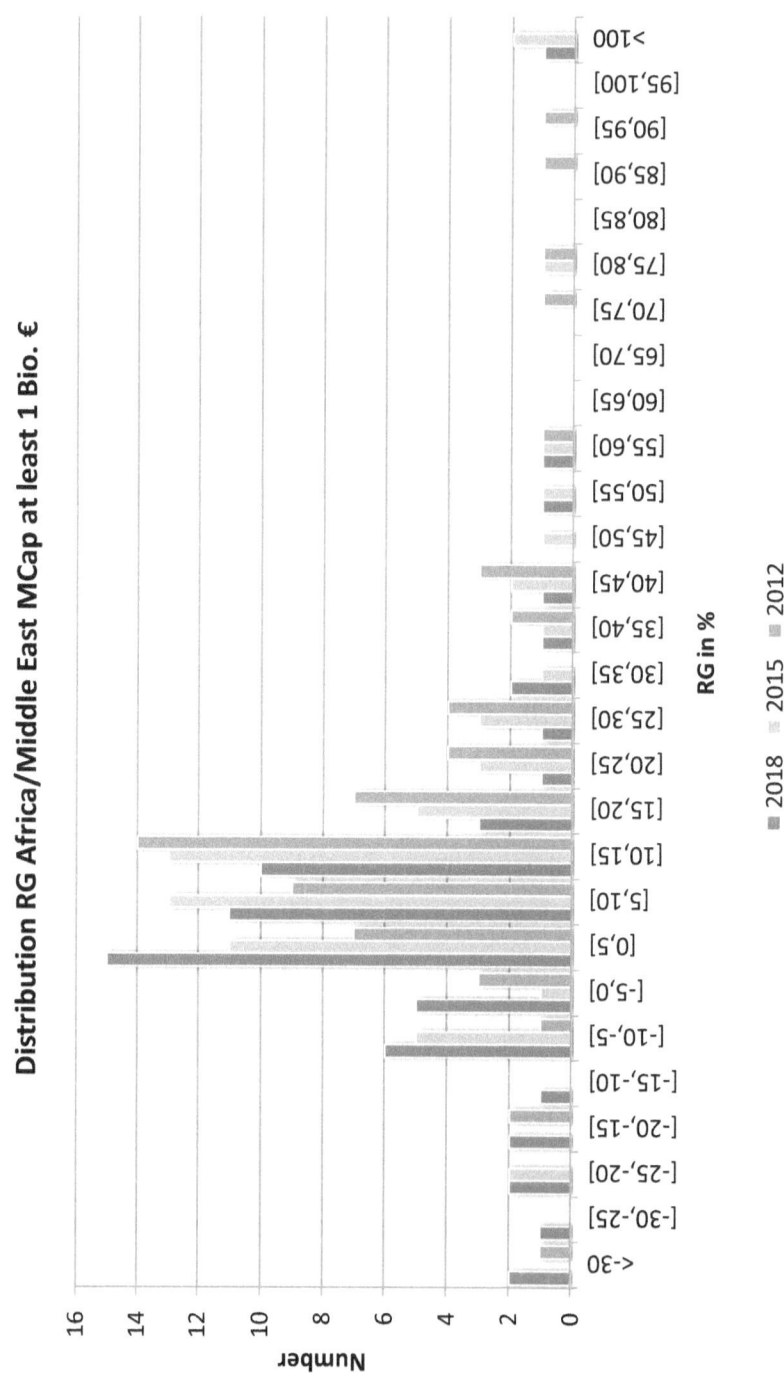

Distribution RG Africa/Middle East MCap at least 1 Bio. €

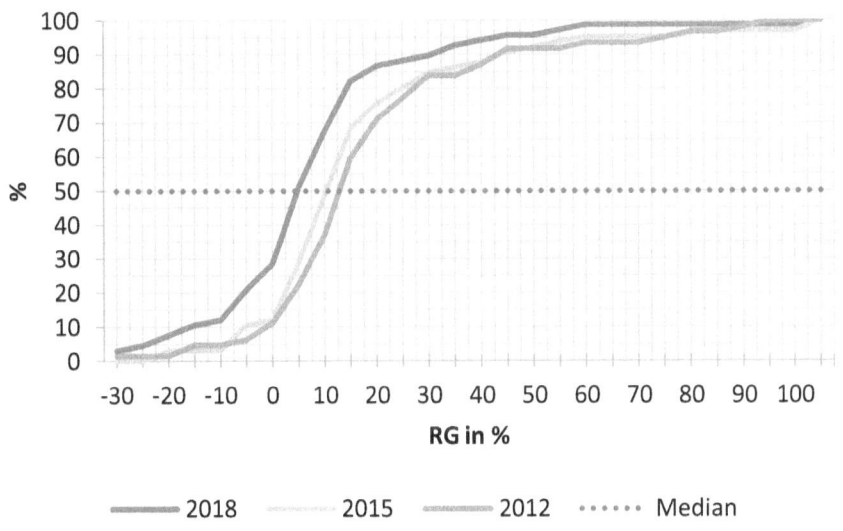

Distribution Function RG Africa/Middle East MCap at least 1 Bio. €

A shift of the distribution and the distribution function to the left can be recognized.

Quartiles RG in % Africa/Middle East (MCap at least 1 Bio. €)			
	2012	2015	2018
lower quartile	7,34	4,36	-2,05
median	12,45	10,40	3,39
upper quartile	22,87	17,83	12,32

If you look at the data on finanzen.net, it can be recognized that the companies with RG values above the median are distributed across all company sizes.

Central and South America

An analogous investigation was carried out for the region Central and South America. In contrast to the region Africa/Middle East, no shift in the distribution or the distribution function can be determined here over the period. More companies could be taken as a basis here. Nevertheless, the quartiles show only slight fluctuations. A trend of the quartiles cannot be recognized.

Quartiles RG in % Middle and South America (MCap at least 1 Bio. €)			
	2012	2015	2018
unteres Quartil	8,57	0,205	3,74
Median	13,16	10,08	11,56
oberes Quartil	24,73	19,59	24,29

Only the lower quartile shows greater fluctuations. The distribution functions are therefore very close together.

If you compare the medians with those of the region Africa/Middle East, there are only few differences.

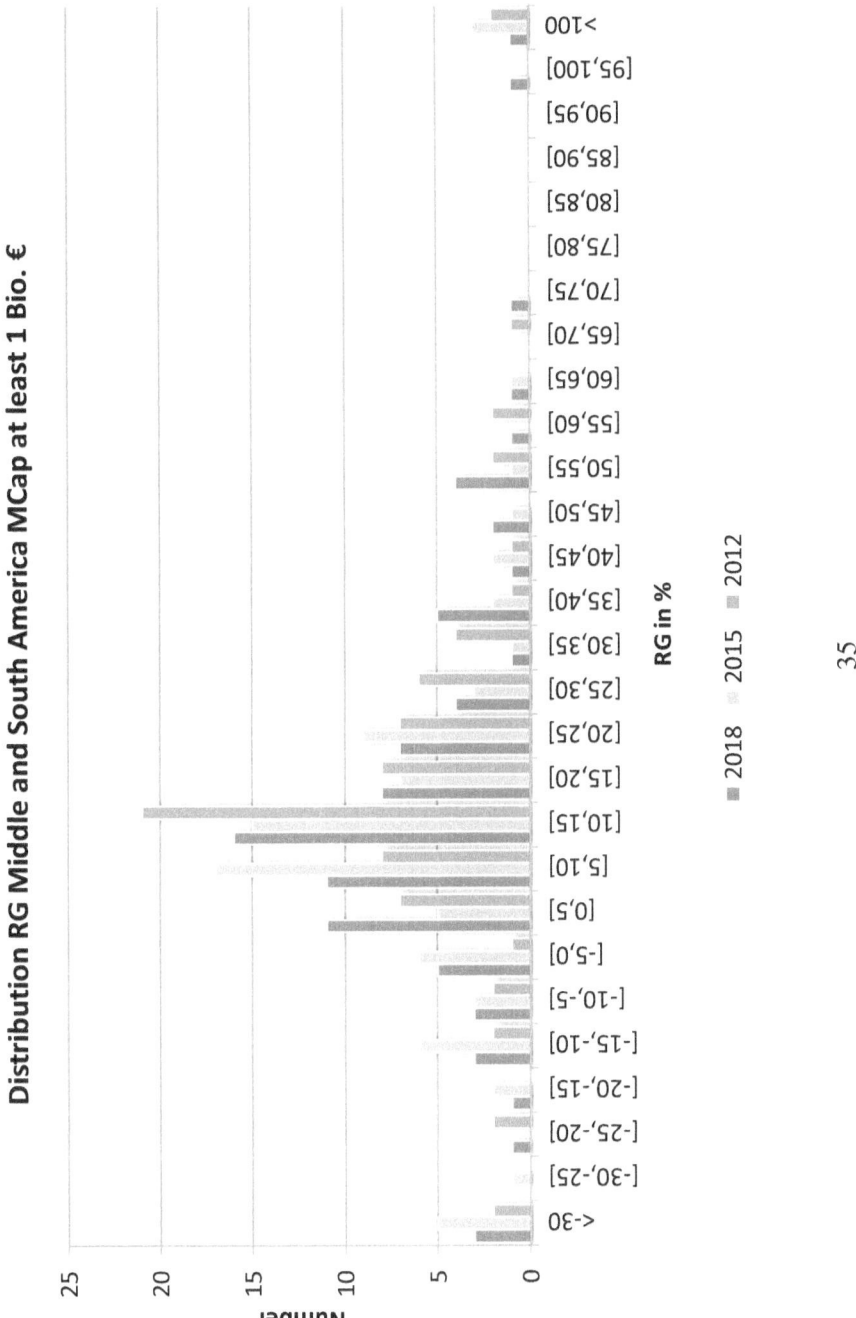

Distribution RG Middle and South America MCap at least 1 Bio. €

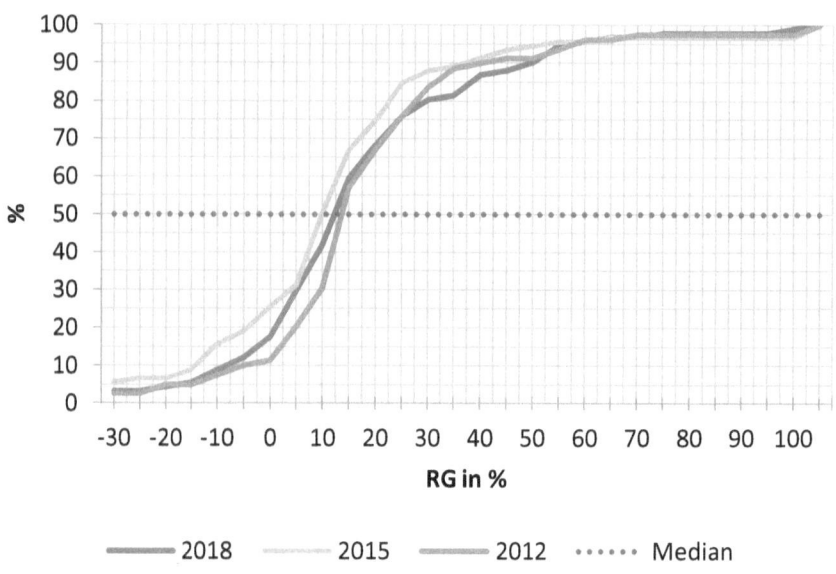

Distribution Function RG Middle and South America MCap at least 1 Bio. €

Asia/Pacific

The region Asia Pacific will provide significantly more companies. I want to set a maximum of 100 companies. If I do the same method as for the other two regions, I would very likely only find the largest 100 companies. The reader (and myself too) may not only be interested in large companies. At the same time, it could be of interest to find potential investments. The list of these 100 companies can be found in the attachment. I will therefore install another filter. This must be taken into account in all analyzes, in which the quartiles determined below are included.

Because Onvista can show profit growth for most companies in this region, I choose the profit growth as the additional filter. Because I am referring to 2018 with a minimum market capitalization of 1 billion €, I will also apply the additional filter to this year. I demand a value that is just below the median of 7%. A profit growth of at least 5 % should be the additional filter.

The following results were achieved:

Quartiles RG in % Asia/Pacific (MCap at least 1 Bio. €)			
	2012	2015	2018
lower quartile	2,51	-0,94	1,77
median	12,41	5,93	8,27
upper quartile	20,87	15,29	17,76

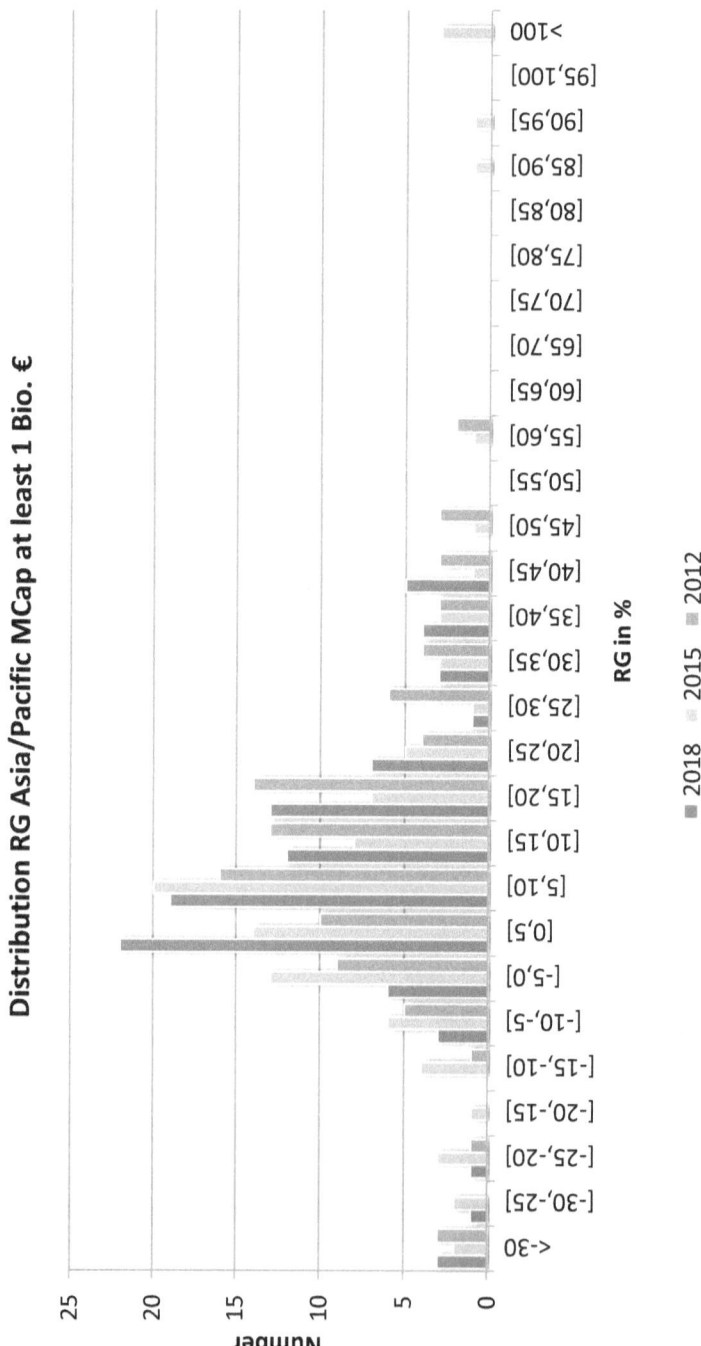

Distribution RG Asia/Pacific MCap at least 1 Bio. €

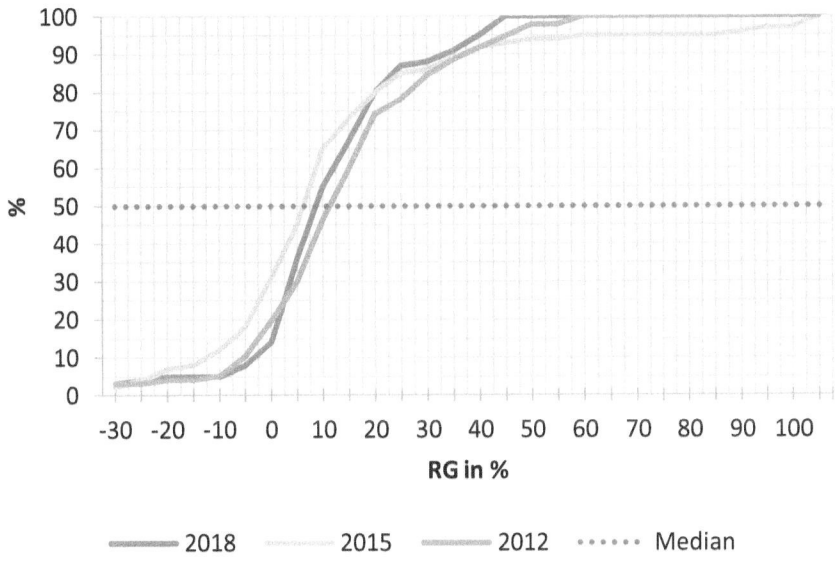

Distribution Function RG Asia/Pacific MCap at least 1 Bio. €

For comparison purposes, the RG quartiles of the industrialized countries are given here[21]: -2.5% / 3.6% / 10%.

Revenue Growth Continuity

The available data makes it possible to list all companies that exceed the RG median in every single year from 2012 to 2018. The data can also be used to list all companies in the respective region that could not exceed the median only in one year of the period.

---

[21] Cf. WALTHER(2019), p.31

RG-Median from 2012 to 2018 fulfilled in every year

Africa/Middle East: RG-Median from 2012 to 2018 fulfilled			
WKN	Company	Business Sector	Ctr
779555	Capitec Bank	Bank	ZAF
902130	Commercial International Bank	Bank	EGY[22]
A1W7AU	Wix.com	Website Modula	ISR[23]
A12CPP	Cyber-Ark Software	Information Security	ISR
A1W3GY	Plus500	Financial Service	ISR

Middle and South America: RG-Median from 2012 to 2018 fulfilled			
WKN	Company	Business Sector	Ctr
A0MNX4	Country Garden	Real Estate	KYM
A0HNNB	Minth Group	Automotive	KYM
A1W2NH	Chinasoft International	IT	KYM

Asia/Pacific: RG-Median from 2012 to 2018 fulfilled			
WKN	Company	Business Sector	Ctr
A1138D	Tencent	Internet service	HKG
694482	HDFC Bank	Bank	IND
891239	Sm Prime	Tourism / Leisure	PHL
A12GJC	Rakuten	Internet commerce	JPN

---

[22] EGY - Egypt
[23] ISR - Israel

RG-Median not fulfilled in one out of the years from 2012 to 2018

Africa/Middle East: RG-Median from 2012 to 2018 fulfilled			
WKN	Company	Business Sector	Ctr
A0LETJ	Exxaro Resources	Energy/Raw Materials	ZAF
A1C3UJ	Makemytrip	Tourism/Leisure	MUS[24]

Middle and South America: RG-Median from 2012 to 2018 fulfilled			
WKN	Company	Business Sector	Ctr
A2APDK	China Evergrande Group	Real Estate	KYM
A0MYNP	MercadoLibre	Internet commerce	ARG
A1KAGA	Deutsche Bank Mexico	Bank	MEX
A2ACSB	Genscript Biotech	Biotechnology	KYM
A1W546	IGG	Software/Internet	KYM
A1XADU	Fo Shou Yuan International	Health Care	KYM

Asia/Pacific: RG-Median from 2012 to 2018 fulfilled			
WKN	Company	Business Sector	Ctr
A0M4YR	Ping An Insurance	Insurance	CHN
919668	Infosys	Software/Internet	IND
891638	Fast Retailing	Retail Trade	JPN
A0F452	Oversea Chinese Banking	Bank	SGP
A0NACD	China Pacific Insurance	Insurance	CHN
A0M4SZ	Poly Real Estate Group	Real Estate Developm.	CHN
A0CACX	Geely	Vehicle Manufacturer	CHN

---

[24] MUS - Mauritius

857627	Taisei	Construction Business	JPN
A0CBDJ	Sino Biopharmaceutical	Pharma	HKG
863403	Santos	Oil and Gas	AUS

Overall, companies from different countries made it onto the lists. If you look at the business sectors, then certain concentrations can be determined. In particular, banks and financial service providers, as well as software and internet companies appear relatively frequently in these lists.

Chapter 4: Equity Ratio

I will now repeat the investigation method, carried out for revenue growth in the previous chapter, on the equity ratio. To do this, I will look at exact the same companies that were analyzed for the revenue growth.

First, I list the dynamic quartiles of the three regions determined by the analysis, whereby it can be seen that these ER quartiles are significantly less dynamic than the RG quartiles from the previous chapter. Keep in mind that the same companies were considered as in the revenue growth analysis.

Quartiles ER in % Africa/Middle East (MCap at least 1 Bio. €)			
	2012	2015	2018
lower quartile	18,61	20,85	23
median	43,86	41,57	42,66
upper quartile	62,39	59,47	62,78

Quartiles ER in % Central/South America (MCap at least 1 Bio. €)			
	2012	2015	2018
lower quartile	24,46	23,31	23,23
median	41,76	36,64	44,75
upper quartile	61,9	61,61	63,01

Quartiles ER in % Asia/Pacific (MCap at least 1 Bio. €)			
	2012	2015	2018
lower quartile	22,30	20,29	22,55
median	43,81	43,00	44,35
upper quartile	64,33	63,89	60,41

Due to these slight fluctuations, it seems to me to be sufficient if the ER distribution is only shown for one single year, in this case 2018. For this I present the three regions in one diagram for the distribution or the distribution function. This ensures better comparability.

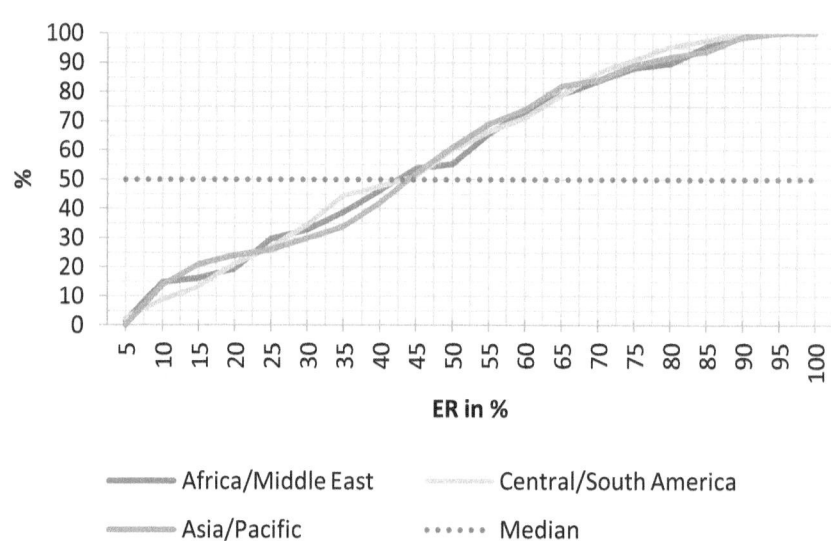

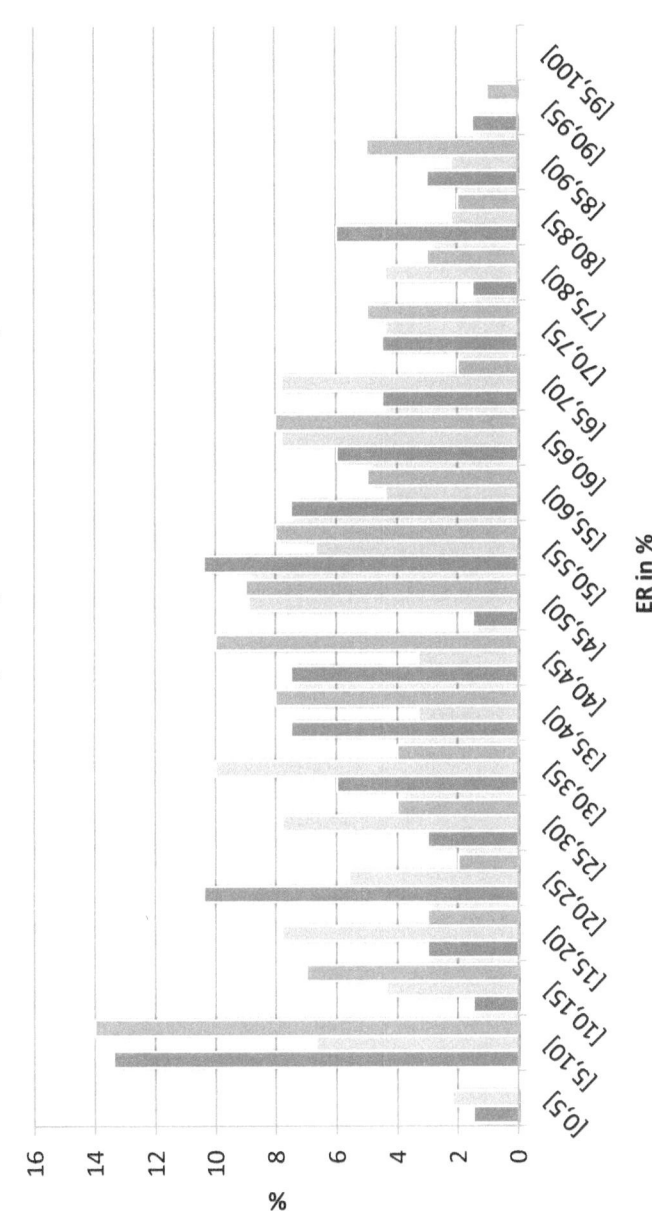

Distribution ER (MCap at least 1 Bio. €)

45

The flat and wide distributions and the almost linear distribution functions suggest roughly an equal distribution of the ER.

I am now finding out which companies were permanently able to show an ER above the dynamic ER median in the period between 2012 and 2018.

Africa/Middle East: Companies with ER from 2012 to 2018 above ER-Median			
WKN	Company	Business Sector	Ctr.
906614	Naspers	Entertainment electronics	ZAF
865164	Sasol	Other Energy/Raw materials	ZAF
901638	Check Point Software	Standard software	ISR
856547	Anglo American Platinum	Raw materials	ZAF
907557	RMB	Financial service	ZAF
578937	Remgro	Holding	ZAF
A0MK4E	Mellanox Technologies	Semiconductor	ISR
A1J0BT	Mr. Price Group	Clothing/Sportswear/ Household	ZAF
A0F69Z	Tiger Brands	Food	ZAF
A0LETJ	Exxaro Resources	Raw materials	ZAF
897505	Taro Pharmaceutical	Pharma	ISR
A1C4AY	Assore	Synthetics	ZAF
A12CPP	Cyber-Ark Software	IT-Security	ISR
914428	Truworths International	Clothin	ZAF
784554	AVI	Food	ZAF
A0CAQD	African Rainbow Minerals	Mining	ZAF
A1W3GY	Plus500	Online services	ISR
A0KFSB	Impala Platinum	Precious metals	ZAF

		Real Estate/Energy/...	QAT
A0KD6M	United Development Comp.		
A117WT	Hyprop Investments	Real Estate	ZAF
A0HM5H	Telecom Egypt	Telecommunication	EGY
A1CTH2	Pioneer Foods Group	Packaging	ZAF

Middle and South America: Companies with ER from 2012 to 2018 above ER-Median			
WKN	Company	Business Sector	Ctr.
A14PRL	Wal-Mart de Mexico	Services	MEX
A0HL4U	Shenzhou International Group	Clothing	KYM
A1KAGA	Deutsche Bank Mexico	Bank	MEX
A0MVDZ	Anta Sports Products	Sportswear	KYM
A1JBMK	Arca Continental	Beverage	MEX
A1CVRA	El Puerto de Liverpool	Services	MEX
885075	Grupo Carso	Services	MEX
A1JQKP	Chow Tai Fook Jewellery	Conglomerate	KYM
A1J083	AAC Technologies	Telecommunication-technology	KYM
A0HNNB	Minth Group	Automotive	KYM
A1T7KW	CIBanco	Bank	MEX
A0LGD0	Haitian International	Synthetics	KYM
910253	Corporacion Moctezuma	Construction materials	MEX
A1C6AA	SITC International	Logistics	KYM
A0H1Q1	Copa	Airline	PAN
A1JLYP	China Medical System	Pharma	KYM
A14VQ9	SSY Group	Pharma	KYM

A0M412	Bosideng International	Clothing	KYM
A0MW2Y	Industrias Bachoco	Poultry	MEX
A0EABF	Grupo Gigante	Services	MEX
A0Q2S5	Fabrinet	Elektronics	KYM
909187	Gerdau	Metalworking	BRA
A12GJT	Xiabuxiabu Catering	Restaurants	KYM
936016	Sunevision	Services	KYM
A0ER8B	Guararapes Confeccoes	Textile industry	BRA
A1W2NH	Chinasoft International	Cloud computing	KYM
907440	SA	Services	KYM
A1J58B	Ambarella	Semiconductor	KYM

Asia/Pacific: Companies with ER from 2012 to 2018 above ER-Median			
WKN	Company	Business Sector	Ctr.
888322	Samsung	Entertainment electronics	KOR[25]
A0B846	CNOOC	Oil and gas	CHN
919668	Infosys	Special software	IND
902427	Lukoil Oil Company	Oil and gas	RUS
892536	PT Hanjaya Mandala Samp.	Beverage/tobacco	IDN[26]
A12BJJ	Recruit	Services	HKG
861270	Sun Hung Kai Properties	Real Estate	HKG
853055	Canon	Other technology	JPN
857031	Kao	Drug Store/cosmetics	JPN
857216	Chugai Pharmaceutical	Pharma	JPN

[25] KOR – South Korea
[26] IDN - Indonesia

579779	MTR	Railway/Street	HKG
A0HHH9	Galaxy Entertainment Group	Casinos	HKG
A0J4TC	Gazprom Neft	Oil and gas	RUS
A1CXQA	Swire Properties	Real Estate	HKG
891239	Sm Prime	Tourism/leisure	PHL
863807	Unicharm	Drug Store/cosmetics	JPN
956202	Sk Telecom	Telecommunication prov.	KOR
865510	Tokyo Electron	Semiconductor	JPN
955991	Hyundai Mobis	Automotive supplier	KOR
877047	Hongkong Land	Holdings	HKG
860990	Swire Pacific	Holdings	HKG
A0M5NZ	Shanghai International Airport	Airport	CHN
923086	Samsung SDI	Electro-technology	KOR
865682	Shimano	Other consumer goods	JPN
A0JD4G	Inpex	Raw materials	JPN
A0M4YQ	PetroChina	Oil and gas	CHN
885677	Kia Motors	Automobile production	KOR
866305	Sino Land	Financial Service	HKG
A1JPFB	Nexon	Gaming	JPN
A1J0X1	IHH Healthcare Bhd	Health Care	MYS[27]
888037	PT United Tractors	Mechanical Engineering	IND
858523	Kyowa Hakko Kogyo	Pharma	JPN
915793	Trend Micro	Special software	JPN
A0MYD2	PT Semen Gresik (Persero)	Baumaterial/komponenten	IND

---

[27] MYS - Malaysia

A1H8S1	Treasury Wine Estates	Wein	AUS
853783	Asahi Glass	Sonstige Technologie	JPN
A0M4XS	China Telecom	Telekomdienstleister	CHN

Chapter 5: Dividend Dynamics

In this chapter, I will filter out of the already known amount of companies those, which have a continuous dividend increase. Only companies that have paid a dividend since at least 2013 and that have neither canceled nor decreased are listed. I take the data from finanzen.net. Any special dividends may result in excluding companies, because the change in the dividend per share in the following year of a year with a special dividend could have been negative. The tables show the respective median dividend increase from 2012 to 2018, from 2014 to 2018, and from 2016 to 2018. It should also be noted that only the period from 2012 to 2018 was considered. Changes in dividends outside this period could not be identified for all companies with the help of the common internet platforms. Companies that do not pay dividends were also excluded from the investigation.

Africa/Middle East

WKN	Company	average. Div.-Chg. in %			Ctr.
		12-18	14-18	16-18	
A1WZEW	Firstrand	20,7	12,8	7,8	ZAF
A0NEF6	Standard Bank Group	12,7	12,7	15,7	ZAF
A0M6V0	DP World	9,5	7,9	7,9	ARE
A0HGK5	Sanlam	9,4	8,9	8,2	ZAF
A2JE9V	Barclays Africa Group	3,9	3,9	3,7	ZAF
907557	RMB	21,3	10,9	7,3	ZAF
578937	Remgro	8,7	8,7	8,4	ZAF

A1J0BT	Mr. Price Group	15	6,2	3,9	ZAF
A0ET80	Aspen Pharmacare	14,9	14,9	14,8	ZAF
904857	PSP Group	25	25	10,7	ZAF
A0F69Z	Tiger Brands	1,8	1,4	1,4	ZAF
A0RPRJ	Clicks Group	18	18	18	ZAF
A0DKNA	Spar Group	11,3	8	5,2	ZAF
932568	Network Healthcare	9,5	9,5	3,3	ZAF
784554	AVI	11,5	10,7	9,5	ZAF
A0MSAR	Santam	8,1	8,1	8	ZAF
A1W3GY	Plus500	26,8	26,8	26,8	ISR
912732	Blom Bank	13,3	19,7	13,3	LBN[28]

18 of the 67 companies in the region Africa/Middle East can meet the conditions. If you look at the medians, it is more likely that the dividend dynamics are declining. On the one hand, all companies are highlighted in which all three medians are above an average dividend increase of 10%. On the other hand, all companies are marked for which the median value of the dividend increase does not decrease. A total of 6 companies meet this requirement.

---

[28] LBN - Lebanon

Central and South America

Only 14 of the 91 companies in the region Central and South America can show the required at least non-negative dividend dynamic. Here, too, I would like to highlight all companies (in this case 8) that, like for the region Africa/Middle East, meet the above-mentioned conditions.

WKN	Company	average. Div.-Chg. in %			Ctr.
		12-18	14-18	16-18	
903621	China Resources Land	28,4	22,7	28,4	KYM
A0HL4U	Shenzhou International Group	20,7	20,7	20,7	KYM
A1KAGA	Deutsche Bank Mexico	7,6	3,4	3,4	MEX
724594	Grupo Elektra	9,4	9,4	25	MEX
A1JBMK	Arca Continental	5,7	8,1	8,1	MEX
900573	Grupo Financie. Inburs.	4,8	4,6	4,4	MEX
885075	Grupo Carso	4,8	2,3	2,2	MEX
894814	Kimberly-Clark d. Mexico	5,7	4	2,7	MEX
896739	Bancolombia	7	7	7,1	COL[29]
904122	Grupo Televisa	0	0	0	MEX
A1W6CU	Nexteer Automotive Group	23,3	23,3	17,5	KYM
A0RM2N	China Zhongwang	19,1	19,1	19,1	KYM
A1JLYP	China Medical System	28,5	28,5	28,5	KYM
936016	Sunevision	10,2	8,7	8,7	KYM

---

[29] COL - Colombia

Asia/Pacific

For the region Asia/Pacific, 37 out of the 100 companies could be filtered out, which showed a non-negative dividend dynamic in the period under review. 29 of these companies received a mark, although it must be mentioned that 10 of these companies have at least 2 medians with a 0% dividend growth.

WKN	Company	average. Div.-Chg. in %			Ctr.
		12-18	14-18	16-18	
A1138D	Tencent	30,6	30,6	29,8	HKG
888322	Samsung	45,5	39,9	49,1	KOR
A2JG9Z	Broadcom	42,9	41,3	71,6	SGP[30]
873029	Nippon	14,3	20	20	JPN
694482	HDFC Bank	18,2	16,8	15,8	IND
A0M4YR	Ping An Insurance	33,3	33,3	36,8	CHN
919668	Infosys	13,5	9	6,2	IND
902427	Lukoil Oil Company	16,3	14,9	10,3	RUS
891638	Fast Retailing	11,5	3,5	0	JPN
880105	DBS Group	3,5	3,5	29	SGP
861270	Sun Hung Kai Properties	0	6,5	13,4	HKG
358693	PT Unilever Indonesia	9,6	9	9,6	IDN
884705	China Overseas Land Investm.	17	12,5	12,5	HKG
853055	Canon	0	0	0	JPN
A0F452	Oversea Chinese Banking	3	2,8	2,8	SGP
878618	United Overseas Bank	4,7	4,7	4,7	SGP
676056	Kaikornbank	0	0	0	THA[31]

[30] SGP - Singapore
[31] THA - Thailand

A0M4W0	Bank of Communications	0	0	0	CHN
A1CXQA	Swire Properties	8,5	8,5	8,5	HKG
956202	Sk Telecom	0	0	0	KOR
853764	Asahi Group	12	11,1	32	JPN
876478	Familymart	3,8	3,8	1,8	JPN
877047	Hongkong Land	5,6	5,3	5,3	HKG
865682	Shimano	16	0	0	JPN
A0JD4G	Inpex	0	0	0	JPN
866305	Sino Land	2	0	2	HKG
A1J0X1	IHH Healthcare Bhd	0	0	0	MYS
858523	Kyowa Hakko Kogyo	0	0	8	JPN
914702	Don Quijote	11,1	18,2	23,1	JPN
857627	Taisei	25	25	25	JPN
A0B5GC	Techtronic Industries	32,6	30,4	30,4	CHN
A12GJC	Rakuten	0	0	0	JPN
874338	Ramsay Health Care	17,5	17,8	13	AUS
A1H8S1	Treasury Wine Estates	23,1	23,1	30	AUS
A0M4XS	China Telecom	8,7	8,7	9,5	CHN
889570	PT Indah Kiat Pulp Paper	0	0	20	IDN
A1C3PC	San Miguel	0	0	0	PHL

A total of 43 companies were marked.

For a dividend investor there is obviously a wide range of countries in which he could invest in the emerging markets. After all, 25 companies were found whose average annual dividend increase is at least 10%.

Attachment

Attachements Chapter 1

Distribution P/E

Africa/Middle East					
P/E	2016	2017	2018	$\bar{x}^{32}$	cum. part.
[0,5]	37	35	50	41	29,7
[5,10]	19	18	41	26	48,5
[10,15]	27	26	36	30	70,2
[15,20]	13	18	23	18	83,2
[20,25]	6	11	11	9	89,7
[25,30]	0	5	6	4	92,6
[30,35]	0	2	0	1	93,3
[35,40]	3	0	3	2	94,7
[40,45]	0	2	1	1	95,4
[45,50]	0	1	1	1	96,1
[50,55]	0	0	3	1	96,8
[55,60]	0	0	0	0	96,8
[60,65]	0	0	0	0	96,8
[65,70]	1	0	1	1	97,5
[70,75]	0	2	0	1	98,2
[75,80]	0	0	0	0	98,2
[80,85]	0	0	1	0	98,2
[85,90]	0	0	0	0	98,2
[90,95]	1	0	0	0	98,2
[95,100]	0	0	0	0	98,2
>100	1	3	3	2	100

---

[32] The average rounded to an integer is given.

Example: If you want to know what % of the companies fall into class the [**10**|**30**], then the value of the last column of the class [5|**10**] must be subtracted from the value of the last column of the class [25|**30**] : 92.6% - 45.5% = 47.1%. That means 47.1% of companies in this region fall into the class [10|30].

Central and South America					
P/E	2016	2017	2018	x̄	cum. part.
[0,5]	26	24	39	30	15,4
[5,10]	17	47	68	44	38
[10,15]	11	44	50	35	55,9
[15,20]	12	32	38	27	69,7
[20,25]	10	24	18	17	78,4
[25,30]	4	18	16	13	85,1
[30,35]	2	10	10	7	88,7
[35,40]	1	12	6	6	91,8
[40,45]	1	4	5	3	93,3
[45,50]	2	4	2	3	94,8
[50,55]	0	2	2	1	95,3
[55,60]	0	3	1	1	95,8
[60,65]	0	0	2	1	96,3
[65,70]	0	0	1	0	96,3
[70,75]	0	1	0	0	96,3
[75,80]	0	0	0	0	96,3
[80,85]	0	1	1	1	96,8
[85,90]	0	0	1	0	96,8
[90,95]	0	1	1	1	97,3
[95,100]	0	0	0	0	97,3
>100	1	8	7	5	100

Asia/Pacific					
P/E	2016	2017	2018	$\bar{x}$	cum. part-
[0,5]	138	105	221	155	8,2
[5,10]	200	237	543	327	25,4
[10,15]	384	409	579	457	49,5
[15,20]	279	360	369	336	67,2
[20,25]	158	203	225	195	77,5
[25,30]	94	143	126	121	83,9
[30,35]	52	81	71	68	87,5
[35,40]	37	78	51	55	90,4
[40,45]	20	45	32	32	92,1
[45,50]	12	23	17	17	93
[50,55]	11	12	12	12	93,6
[55,60]	11	9	14	11	94,2
[60,65]	11	10	6	9	94,7
[65,70]	10	3	7	7	95,1
[70,75]	12	10	5	9	95,6
[75,80]	7	5	7	6	95,9
[80,85]	6	4	2	4	96,1
[85,90]	9	7	6	7	96,5
[90,95]	7	6	4	6	96,8
[95,100]	1	1	4	2	96,9
>100	73	64	53	63	100

Distribution P/CF

Africa/Middle East					
P/CF	2016	2017	2018	$\bar{x}$	cum. part.
<-20	1	1	0	1	1,3
[-20,-15]	0	0	0	0	1,3
[-15,-10]	1	0	2	1	2,6
[-10,-5]	0	0	1	0	2,6
[-5,0]	6	8	10	8	12,6
[0,5]	19	18	31	23	41,4
[5,10]	15	20	32	22	68,9
[10,15]	6	13	18	12	83,9
[15,20]	5	3	8	5	90,2
[20,25]	1	3	3	2	92,7
[25,30]	1	1	2	1	94
[30,35]	0	1	0	0	94
[35,40]	0	1	1	1	95,3
[40,45]	1	1	1	1	96,6
[45,50]	1	0	2	1	97,9
>50	1	1	3	2	100

Central and South America					
P/CF	2016	2017	2018	$\bar{x}_{17/18}$	cum. part.
<-20	1	7	14	11	5,8
[-20,-15]	0	1	17	9	10,5
[-15,-10]	2	3	4	4	12,6
[-10,-5]	0	1	3	2	13,6
[-5,0]	4	9	10	10	18,8
[0,5]	15	15	39	27	32,9
[5,10]	9	28	51	40	53,8
[10,15]	10	31	36	34	71,6
[15,20]	5	15	20	18	81
[20,25]	4	10	7	9	85,7
[25,30]	1	14	7	11	91,5
[30,35]	2	2	3	3	93,1
[35,40]	0	1	3	2	94,1
[40,45]	0	1	1	1	94,6
[45,50]	0	1	0	1	95,1
>50	0	9	8	9	100

Asia/Pacific					
P/CF	2016	2017	2018	$\bar{x}$	cum. part.
<-20	23	42	51	39	2,8
[-20,-15]	1	5	17	8	3,4
[-15,-10]	10	7	13	10	4,1
[-10,-5]	7	11	25	14	5,1
[-5,0]	47	42	69	53	8,9
[0,5]	208	186	380	258	27,2
[5,10]	307	319	506	377	53,9
[10,15]	239	255	308	267	72,8
[15,20]	122	161	192	158	84
[20,25]	53	109	97	86	90,1
[25,30]	31	46	37	38	92,8
[30,35]	19	32	28	26	94,6
[35,40]	9	17	16	14	95,6
[40,45]	8	8	8	8	96,2
[45,50]	11	9	2	7	96,7
>50	42	50	57	50	100

Africa/Middle East	MCap in Bio. €										
		[0,1]	[1,2]	[2,3]	[3,4]	[4,5]	[5,6]	[6,7]	[7,8]	[8,9]	[9,10]	>10
P/E	[0,5]	43	2	0	2	2	0	0	0	0	0	1
	[5,10]	25	7	3	1	1	1	1	0	2	0	0
	[10,15]	18	7	3	1	1	0	2	0	0	0	4
	[15,20]	9	2	3	2	2	1	2	0	1	0	2
	[20,25]	0	1	3	2	2	0	0	1	0	0	2
	[25,30]	3	0	0	0	0	0	0	0	0	0	2
	[30,35]	1	1	1	0	0	0	0	0	0	0	0
	[35,40]	1	0	0	0	0	0	0	0	0	0	0
	[40,45]	0	0	1	0	0	0	0	0	0	0	0
	[45,50]	3	0	0	0	0	0	0	0	0	0	0
	[50,55]	0	0	0	0	0	0	0	0	0	0	0
	[55,60]	0	0	0	0	0	0	0	0	0	0	0
	[60,65]	0	0	0	0	0	0	0	0	0	0	0
	[65,70]	1	0	0	0	0	0	0	0	0	0	0
	[70,75]	0	0	0	0	0	0	0	0	0	0	0
	[75,80]	0	0	0	1	0	0	0	0	0	0	0
	[80,85]	0	0	0	0	0	0	0	0	0	0	0
	[85,90]	0	0	0	0	0	0	0	0	0	0	0
	[90,95]	0	0	0	0	0	0	0	0	0	0	0
	[95,100]	0	0	0	0	0	0	0	0	0	0	0
	>100	4	0	0	0	0	0	0	0	0	0	0

VI

Central and South America	MCap in Bio. €										
P/E	[0,1]	[1,2]	[2,3]	[3,4]	[4,5]	[5,6]	[6,7]	[7,8]	[8,9]	[9,10]	>10
[0,5]	28	5	2	1	1	2	0	0	0	0	0
[5,10]	30	13	7	2	3	4	1	0	0	0	7
[10,15]	20	12	8	1	0	1	1	1	4	0	2
[15,20]	16	9	4	2	3	0	0	1	0	1	0
[20,25]	6	4	1	1	1	1	0	0	1	1	2
[25,30]	5	6	3	1	0	0	0	0	0	0	1
[30,35]	5	1	1	1	1	0	0	0	1	0	0
[35,40]	2	0	1	0	3	0	0	0	0	0	0
[40,45]	3	0	1	0	0	0	0	0	0	0	1
[45,50]	1	1	0	0	0	0	0	0	0	0	0
[50,55]	0	1	0	0	0	0	0	0	0	0	0
[55,60]	0	0	1	0	0	0	0	0	0	0	0
[60,65]	1	1	0	0	0	0	0	0	0	0	0
[65,70]	1	0	0	0	0	0	0	0	0	0	0
[70,75]	0	0	0	0	0	0	0	0	0	0	0
[75,80]	0	0	0	0	0	0	0	0	0	0	0
[80,85]	1	0	0	0	0	0	0	1	0	0	0
[85,90]	0	0	0	0	0	1	0	0	0	0	0
[90,95]	0	0	0	0	0	0	0	0	0	0	0
[95,100]	0	0	0	0	0	0	0	0	0	0	0
>100	4	3	1	0	0	0	0	1	0	0	0

VII

Asia/Pacific	MCap in Bio. €										
		[0,1]	[1,2]	[2,3]	[3,4]	[4,5]	[5,6]	[6,7]	[7,8]	[8,9]	[9,10]	>10
P/E	[0,5]	116	26	14	6	5	3	3	3	3	2	12
	[5,10]	263	74	40	35	19	10	5	8	5	6	70
	[10,15]	386	103	34	33	31	7	9	16	9	2	77
	[15,20]	144	61	39	19	15	13	8	15	5	6	36
	[20,25]	79	43	20	15	10	5	7	8	6	3	3
	[25,30]	44	16	10	9	7	7	5	4	5	1	16
	[30,35]	21	11	7	5	4	7	1	3	2	1	8
	[35,40]	17	11	3	2	3	1	1	0	0	0	11
	[40,45]	15	5	2	3	2	1	1	0	0	0	2
	[45,50]	6	2	1	3	0	2	0	1	0	1	1
	[50,55]	4	1	0	2	0	0	0	2	0	0	1
	[55,60]	5	2	1	4	1	1	0	0	0	0	0
	[60,65]	2	1	0	1	0	1	1	0	0	0	0
	[65,70]	4	0	0	0	0	0	0	0	0	0	2
	[70,75]	0	1	1	0	0	1	0	1	0	0	1
	[75,80]	4	0	0	0	0	1	0	0	0	0	0
	[80,85]	1	0	1	0	0	0	0	0	0	0	0
	[85,90]	5	0	0	0	0	1	0	0	0	0	0
	[90,95]	3	1	0	0	0	0	0	0	0	0	0
	[95,100]	2	0	0	0	1	1	0	0	0	0	0
	>100	30	9	3	2	4	0	1	1	0	0	2

VIII

Attachments Chapter 2

Distribution PG

Africa/Middle East					
PG	2016	2017	2018	x̄	cum. part.
<-100	0	0	0	0	0
[-100,-90]	10	5	0	5	1,9
[-90,-80]	1	2	2	2	2,6
[-80,-70]	5	3	5	4	4,1
[-70,-60]	0	7	5	4	5,6
[-60,-50]	6	13	9	9	8,9
[-50,-40]	7	8	8	8	11,9
[-40,-30]	9	9	12	10	15,6
[-30,-20]	12	11	15	13	20,4
[-20,-10]	32	14	21	22	28,6
[-10,0]	21	35	31	29	39,4
[0,10]	42	51	58	50	58
[10,20]	47	49	32	43	74
[20,30]	10	15	17	14	79,2
[30,40]	7	4	5	5	81,1
[40,50]	4	9	15	9	84,4
[50,60]	10	2	7	6	86,6
[60,70]	1	9	4	5	88,5
[70,80]	5	1	4	3	89,6
[80,90]	1	0	4	2	90,3
[90,100]	0	5	1	2	91
>100	26	23	22	24	100

Central and South America					
PG	2016	2017	2018	$\bar{x}$	cum. part.
<-100	0	0	0	0	0
[-100,-90]	6	18	15	13	3,1
[-90,-80]	14	18	10	14	6,4
[-80,-70]	11	9	5	8	8,3
[-70,-60]	9	8	8	8	10,2
[-60,-50]	8	4	8	7	11,8
[-50,-40]	18	7	14	13	14,9
[-40,-30]	17	15	16	16	18,7
[-30,-20]	23	19	20	21	23,6
[-20,-10]	25	25	26	25	29,5
[-10,0]	36	32	50	39	38,7
[0,10]	53	59	64	59	52,6
[10,20]	38	41	41	40	62
[20,30]	32	29	40	34	70
[30,40]	24	17	21	21	74,9
[40,50]	8	13	9	10	77,3
[50,60]	5	13	2	7	78,9
[60,70]	5	13	11	10	81,3
[70,80]	8	10	15	11	83,9
[80,90]	3	9	7	6	85,3
[90,100]	5	5	5	5	86,5
>100	48	57	70	58	100

X

Asia/Pacific					
PG	2016	2017	2018	$\bar{x}$	cum. part.
<-100	0	0	0	0	0
[-100,-90]	51	57	41	50	1,3
[-90,-80]	69	71	40	60	2,8
[-80,-70]	48	37	39	41	3,8
[-70,-60]	67	50	76	64	5,4
[-60,-50]	72	70	72	71	7,2
[-50,-40]	148	100	64	104	9,8
[-40,-30]	141	100	83	108	12,5
[-30,-20]	216	160	126	167	16,7
[-20,-10]	265	229	160	218	22,2
[-10,0]	449	419	893	587	37,1
[0,10]	574	643	1162	793	57,2
[10,20]	475	474	393	447	68,6
[20,30]	322	313	248	294	76,1
[30,40]	165	206	130	167	80,3
[40,50]	121	122	109	117	83,3
[50,60]	87	118	64	90	85,6
[60,70]	75	87	45	69	87,4
[70,80]	49	66	37	51	88,7
[80,90]	45	48	30	41	89,7
[90,100]	38	43	25	35	90,6
>100	360	476	251	362	100

Central and South America	MCap in Bio. €										
	[0,1]	[1,2]	[2,3]	[3,4]	[4,5]	[5,6]	[6,7]	[7,8]	[8,9]	[9,10]	>10
<-100	0	0	0	0	0	0	0	0	0	0	0
[-100,-90]	9	0	0	0	0	1	0	2	0	0	1
[-90,-80]	3	5	0	0	0	0	0	0	0	1	0
[-80,-70]	3	1	0	0	0	0	0	0	0	0	0
[-70,-60]	7	0	0	1	0	0	0	0	0	0	0
[-60,-50]	6	2	0	0	0	0	0	0	0	0	0
[-50,-40]	7	1	1	0	2	0	0	0	0	0	0
[-40,-30]	8	1	0	0	0	0	1	0	0	1	4
[-30,-20]	6	7	5	0	0	0	2	0	2	0	0
[-20,-10]	9	3	2	3	3	2	0	0	0	0	0
[-10,0]	22	8	3	3	4	1	0	5	0	0	1
[0,10]	27	7	6	3	5	3	0	2	2	1	3
[10,20]	10	10	5	3	2	0	1	4	0	0	4
[20,30]	14	11	3	0	1	0	1	0	1	0	7
[30,40]	8	0	4	2	1	0	0	0	0	0	6
[40,50]	4	2	0	3	0	0	0	0	0	0	0
[50,60]	0	1	0	0	0	0	0	0	0	0	0
[60,70]	1	4	0	0	0	0	1	0	0	0	2
[70,80]	8	0	0	0	4	0	0	0	0	0	0
[80,90]	1	0	0	0	2	0	0	0	0	0	2
[90,100]	2	0	1	0	0	1	0	0	0	0	0
>100	29	12	4	2	2	6	0	3	0	0	1

XIII

Africa/Middle East	MCap in Bio. €										
PG in %	[0,1]	[1,2]	[2,3]	[3,4]	[4,5]	[5,6]	[6,7]	[7,8]	[8,9]	[9,10]	>10
<-100	0	0	0	0	0	0	0	0	0	0	0
[-100,-90]	0	0	0	0	0	0	0	0	0	0	0
[-90,-80]	0	0	0	0	0	0	0	0	0	0	2
[-80,-70]	2	0	0	0	0	0	0	0	0	0	0
[-70,-60]	3	0	0	0	0	0	0	0	0	0	0
[-60,-50]	6	0	0	0	0	0	0	0	0	0	2
[-50,-40]	6	0	0	0	0	0	0	0	0	0	0
[-40,-30]	4	3	2	0	1	0	0	0	0	0	0
[-30,-20]	9	2	0	2	0	0	0	0	0	0	0
[-20,-10]	7	3	0	2	0	0	0	0	0	0	2
[-10,0]	14	5	4	2	0	2	2	0	0	0	1
[0,10]	17	10	9	4	1	1	2	0	2	0	8
[10,20]	9	4	4	1	2	0	1	0	2	0	0
[20,30]	8	2	2	1	3	0	0	1	0	0	0
[30,40]	1	0	0	0	0	0	0	0	0	0	2
[40,50]	7	2	3	0	0	0	0	0	0	0	0
[50,60]	6	0	0	0	0	0	0	0	0	0	0
[60,70]	4	0	0	0	0	0	0	0	0	0	0
[70,80]	3	0	1	0	0	0	0	0	0	0	0
[80,90]	1	0	0	0	0	0	0	0	2	0	2
[90,100]	1	0	0	0	0	0	0	0	0	0	0
>100	13	3	2	4	0	0	0	0	0	0	0

XII

Asia/Pacific	MCap in Bio. €										
	[0,1]	[1,2]	[2,3]	[3,4]	[4,5]	[5,6]	[6,7]	[7,8]	[8,9]	[9,10]	>10
<-100	0	0	0	0	0	0	0	0	0	0	0
[-100,-90]	28	4	1	2	2	0	0	0	0	0	0
[-90,-80]	20	5	2	0	2	1	0	4	0	0	2
[-80,-70]	22	4	5	0	1	0	0	0	1	0	0
[-70,-60]	36	8	3	0	0	3	0	2	0	0	12
[-60,-50]	35	7	12	1	3	2	0	2	0	0	2
[-50,-40]	31	9	2	7	2	0	0	0	0	0	2
[-40,-30]	41	5	4	2	4	2	3	2	4	0	4
[-30,-20]	57	11	11	4	0	6	4	7	2	2	8
[-20,-10]	50	21	19	9	14	0	5	1	3	1	19
[-10,0]	344	128	53	59	46	21	16	34	15	5	122
[0,10]	692	150	76	84	49	40	23	32	11	20	184
[10,20]	98	47	23	11	12	15	9	6	10	0	55
[20,30]	66	19	15	14	13	6	2	3	5	1	30
[30,40]	35	18	6	3	4	0	2	0	4	0	2
[40,50]	32	7	6	8	5	0	5	0	0	0	15
[50,60]	22	6	1	0	2	0	2	2	0	0	10
[60,70]	19	3	2	3	0	0	0	1	0	0	2
[70,80]	15	4	0	1	0	3	0	3	0	0	6
[80,90]	13	2	2	0	0	0	0	0	0	0	3
[90,100]	6	1	2	0	0	0	0	0	0	0	4
>100	125	21	6	5	4	3	1	0	2	0	22

PG in %

XIV

Attachmentes Chapter 3

List of companies: Africa/Middle East

Nr.	WKN	Unternehmen
1	906614	Naspers
2	A1WZEW	Firstrand
3	A0NEF6	Standard Bank Group
4	865164	Sasol
5	883035	Teva
6	A0RM1C	Vodacom Group
7	901638	Check Point Software
8	A0M6V0	DP World
9	A0J3AH	Maroc Telecom
10	A0HGK5	Sanlam
11	897024	MTN Group
12	A2AKNF	Anglo American Platinum
13	A2JE9V	Barclays Africa Group
14	779555	Capitec Bank
15	853202	Shoprite
16	907557	RMB
17	578937	Remgro
18	A0LC6R	Kumbra Iron Ore
19	A2AHEP	BID Corp.
20	902130	Commercial International Bank
21	915102	AngloGold Ashanti
22	A0MK4E	Mellanox Technologies
23	A2JPBS	Pepkor Holdings
24	A0MV5A	Bisvest Group
25	A1W3J7	Growthpoint Properties
26	A0G5BD	Commercial Bank of Qatar
27	A1W7AU	Wix.com
28	A1J0BT	Mr. Price Group
29	A0ET80	Aspen Pharmacare
30	A0D9CN	Woolworth
31	904857	PSP Group
32	A0F69Z	Tiger Brands
33	A0LETJ	Exxaro Resources

34	897505	Taro Pharmaceutical
35	A0RPRJ	Clicks Group
36	860275	Sappi
37	856777	Gold Fields
38	A1C4AY	Assore
39	A0DKNA	Spar Group
40	A12CPP	Cyber-Ark Software
41	914428	Truworths International
42	932568	Network Healthcare
43	A1CZC2	Life Healthcare
44	784554	AVI
45	A0MSAR	Santam
46	875436	Pick'n Pay Stores
47	A0CAQD	African Rainbow Minerals
48	A0RCNQ	Liberty Holdings
49	A1W3GY	Plus500
50	912732	Blom Bank SAL
51	A1107B	Bank Audi
52	A0KFSB	Impala Platinum
53	A2PN0H	Momentum Metropolitan
54	A0KEQC	Investec
55	A2DGS5	Dis-Chem Pharmacies
56	854646	Barloworld
57	A14QVM	Solaredge
58	A1KBRZ	Sibanye Gold
59	A1H5JC	Massmart
60	877208	Northm Platinum
61	893169	Tower Semiconductor
62	A0KD6M	United Development Company
63	A1C3UJ	Makemytrip
64	A117WT	Hyprop Investments
65	A0HM5H	Telecom Egyp
66	A1CTH2	Pioneer Foods Group
67	A1C8E3	Air Arabia PJSC

List of companies: Central and South America

No.	WKN	Company
1	897136	Vale
2	A14PRL	Wal-Mart de Mexico
3	A2APDK	China Evergrande Group
4	A2JNY1	Xiaomi
5	896694	Banco Bradesco
6	903621	China Resources Land
7	A0MNX4	Country Garden
8	A0HL4U	Shenzhou International Group
9	580892	Grupo Mexico
10	907669	Banorte
11	A0YF8N	Sunac China
12	A0MYNP	MercadoLibre
13	A1KAGA	Deutsche Bank Mexico
14	A0MVDZ	Anta Sports Products
15	724594	Grupo Elektra
16	A1JBMK	Arca Continental
17	900573	Grupo Financie. Inburs.
18	904121	Grupo Bimbo
19	A0DNX7	Herbalife
20	925905	Cemex
21	A1CVRA	El Puerto de Liverpool
22	885075	Grupo Carso
23	A1JQKP	Chow Tai Fook Jewellery
24	A1437N	BeiGene
25	A0MNM 2	JBS
26	A2DS7Z	Wuxi Biologics (Cayman)
27	A1J083	AAC Technologies
28	899026	Centrais Electricas Brasileiras
29	A2DNBX	Rumo
30	896720	Alfa
31	A0YHLZ	Cielo
32	A2PBDX	Capri
33	894814	Kimberly-Clark d. Mexico
34	A2PRMA	Mexichem
35	896739	Bancolombia
36	A2DLRY	Becle

37	897910	Industrias Penoles
38	915731	Gruma
39	A0B5M7	Natura Cosmeticos
40	A2H5WZ	China Literature
41	A0MYXF	B2W - Companhia Digital
42	A0ES62	Agile Property
43	A0YGLD	BRF - Brasil Foods
44	A0DNL7	Porto Seguro
45	904122	Grupo Televisa
46	A1142G	Tianhe Chemicals Group
47	A0HNNB	Minth Group
48	A2DTAJ	Health and Happiness Int.
49	A1T7KW	CIBanco
50	A1W6CU	Nexteer Automotive Group
51	A0LGD0	Haitian International
52	910253	Corporacion Moctezuma
53	A2JB7S	PagSeguro Digital
54	A2DT6V	Foxconn Interconnect Techn
55	907398	Organizacion Soriana
56	A1C6AA	SITC International
57	A2ACSB	Genscript Biotech
58	A0H1Q1	Copa
59	A0RM2N	China Zhongwang
60	A0M0Z9	Li Ning Company
61	A1JLYP	China Medical System
62	A2N9M9	Aleatica
63	A14VQ9	SSY Group
64	A1T8GY	Evertec
65	A0M412	Bosideng International
66	A0MW2Y	Industrias Bachoco
67	A0YFP8	Kaisa Group
68	A0EABF	Grupo Gigante
69	A0Q2S5	Fabrinet
70	A0J3NL	Shui On Land
71	899018	Companhia Energetica d. Minas
72	A1W546	IGG
73	909187	Gerdau
74	A12GJT	Xiabuxiabu Catering
75	A1XADU	Fo Shou Yuan International

76	A0M48X	Sul America
77	A1H5FR	Eletropaulo Eletricidade Metr.
78	A1C5AB	MicroPort Scientific
79	A12A8L	China Metal Resources Util.
80	A2H7AY	Yixin Group
81	A1137V	Theravance Biopharma
82	936016	Sunevision
83	A0ER8B	Guararapes Condeccoes
84	A1XBQQ	Gentera
85	A1W2NH	Chinasoft International
86	A2H6WY	Razer
87	A2DJD5	Meitu
88	907440	SA
89	A1J58B	Ambarella
90	A1J025	China Yongda Automobiles
91	A0M61Y	GCL-Poly Energy

List of companies: Asia/Pacific

No.	WKN	Company
1	A1138D	Tencent
2	888322	Samsung
3	A2JG9Z	Broadcom
4	873029	Nippon
5	694482	HDFC Bank
6	A0J3N5	Rosneft
7	A0B846	CNOOC
8	A0M4YR	Ping An Insurance
9	A1JB8N	Sberbank of Russia
10	919668	Infosys
11	902427	Lukoil Oil Company
12	891638	Fast Retailing
13	892536	PT Hanjaya Mandala Samp.
14	870564	CITIC Pacific
15	880105	DBS Group
16	862271	Hang Seng Bank
17	A12BJJ	Recruit
18	861270	Sun Hung Kai Properties
19	661725	Bank of China (Hongkong)
20	358693	PT Unilever Indonesia
21	884705	China Overseas Land Investm.
22	A14QAZ	CK Hutchison
23	A1JZAG	PT Astra International Tbk
24	853055	Canon
25	857031	Kao
26	A0NJY9	Hong Kong Exchange & Clearing
27	A0M4WZ	Bank of China
28	A0F452	Oversea Chinese Banking
29	A0NACD	China Pacific Insurance
30	857216	Chugai Pharmaceutical
31	A0M4KV	China United Network Comm.
32	579779	MTR
33	878618	United Overseas Bank

34	676056	Kaikornbank
35	A0HHH9	Galaxy Entertainment Group
36	A0M4W0	Bank of Communications
37	A2GSU2	Ck Asset
38	883565	Bangkok Bank
39	A0J4TC	Gazprom Neft
40	854002	Shiseido
41	A0M8JF	China Railway Group
42	853666	Panasonic
43	A1CXQA	Swire Properties
44	891239	Sm Prime
45	863807	UNICHARM
46	A0M4SZ	Poly Real Estate Group
47	956202	Sk Telecom
48	865510	Tokyo Electron
49	853764	Asahi Group
50	876478	Familymart
51	955991	Hyundai Mobi
52	A0CACX	Geely
53	877047	Hongkong Land
54	860990	Swire Pacific
55	A1CXM5	Samsung Life Insurance
56	A0M5NZ	Shanghai International Airport
57	923086	Samsung SDI
58	885799	CIMB Group
59	865682	Shimano
60	A0JD4G	Inpex
61	A0M4YQ	PetroChina
62	A0LEJV	Severstal
63	A0B5T9	China Mengniu Diary
64	885677	Kia Motors
65	863443	Wheelock
66	866305	Sino Land
67	A1JPFB	Nexon
68	A1J0X1	IHH Healthcare Bhd
69	884684	China Resources Enterprise
70	725281	ALROSA
71	A0J2LZ	Thai Beverage
72	888037	PT United Tractors
73	858523	Kyowa Hakko Kogyo

74	862665	Jardine Cycle Carriage
75	914702	Don Quijote
76	A0YA1F	China Taiping Insurance
77	857627	Taisei
78	A0B5GC	Techtronic Industries
79	A14SB9	CIMIC Group
80	A12GJC	Rakuten
81	901652	Aristocrat Leisure
82	784581	China Resources Power
83	548183	CSPC Pharmaceutical
84	A0HNQE	Hana Financial
85	A0CBDJ	Sino Biopharmaceutical
86	874338	Ramsay Health Care
87	A0ML07	Keppel
88	863403	Santos
89	931678	Origin Energy
90	915793	Trend Micro
91	A0MYD2	PT Semen Gresik (Persero)
92	899106	Tingyi (Cayman Islands)
93	A1H8S1	Treasury Wine Estates
94	A0MQ3G	Bank for Foreihn Trade Vnesth.
95	853783	Asahi Glass
96	A0M4XS	China Telecom
97	889570	PT Indah Kiat Pulp Paper
98	922613	KT
99	A1C3PC	San Miguel
100	898321	Cochlear

Literature

WALTHER, B. (2019): Investing Based on Key Performance Indicator Distributions and Survival-Time Analyzes. Tables and Charts for Quantitative Investment Strategies. 1st Edition. Published by Amazon Europe. Printed by Amazon Fulfillment Poland. z o.o., Wroclaw.

www.ingramcontent.com/pod-product-compliance
Lightning Source LLC
Chambersburg PA
CBHW030952240526
45463CB00016B/2509